I0753324

THE LEADER WITHIN

Thomas Droge

Published by Pathfinder Spirit

This publication is designed to provide accurate and authoritative information in regard to the subject matter covered. It is sold with the understanding that neither the author nor the publisher is engaged in rendering medical, psychological, or other professional services. The practices and strategies contained herein may not be suitable for your situation. You should consult with a qualified professional when appropriate.

Cover design by Joe Riley

ISBN: 979-8-9950409-1-0

WWW.THOMASDROGE.COM

First Edition

To Bren, my partner in life, love, laughter, and art. Thank you for putting up with the late nights and weekends, for always being there and believing in me, and for loving the beauty and power of words.

To my boys, Mason and Dylan, you have always been my greatest joy, love, and inspiration. I wrote this book because of you.

To Vinay, my friend who followed his intuition and took a chance on a role that had never existed before. Chief Mindfulness Officer

To every student, client, patient, and teacher: Thank you for helping me find my path in this life. It has been a gift to have the honor of spending time with you.

TABLE OF CONTENTS

Introduction xi

How to Use This Book xv

1: The Way of Listening 1

2: Breaking The Pattern 17

3: Let Go 31

4: Slow is the Fast Way 47

5: Adaptive response 63

6: Define the Field 81

7: Finding Flow 99

8: The Perception Gap 117

9: The Oasis Within 135

10: Reclaiming Your Shadow 157

11: Your North Star 175

12: Finding Rhythm 193

13: The Threshold 209

14: Walking Your Path 229

About the author 245

INTRODUCTION

July 1991. A hot summer day in downtown Boston. I stood in a 200-year-old church surrounded by candles, the echoes of stone arches, and the strange hush that comes when a room filled with people are all trying to be brave at the same time. The priest's voice filled the sanctuary: "Yea, though I walk through the valley of the shadow of death, I shall fear no evil…"

As I walked to the pulpit to give the eulogy at my father's funeral, I thought, I'm twenty-eight years old. And I don't know who I am. I don't know what the next phase of my life is going to be. I realized that although I knew my father, I also didn't know my father.

When I speak, I speak from my heart. I talk about what I loved, what I missed, what I remembered most – three things he emphasized again and again: Be kind. Be caring. Do something in the world that makes other people's lives better.

I pushed away another truth, pulsing beneath my words. A truth that didn't fit neatly into the service. The anger. The frustration. The shock of his dying so young and leaving me to figure it out on my own.

From the pulpit, I looked out and saw that the church was completely full. So many people, many of them strangers. *Who are all these people? Where did they come from?*

After the service, they filed past in the reception line, and each person told me a small story. Not dramatic. Not polished. Just honest.

Your father was with me in a moment when I needed someone. Your father helped me find my way when I was lost. Your father inspired me to do what I thought was impossible. Your father showed up when things were hard. Your father said something that changed the way I saw my life.

This was the ripple. I came to bury my father, to say goodbye. What I witnessed was not a ceremony of loss, but the impact of a life, a glimpse into something larger.

It changed how I saw my life. I walked away knowing that our value lies in our actions; how we walk alongside one another through suffering, burdens, celebrations, and change.

That day, I made a decision to measure my progress every year by one metric: how many people I had connected with in some meaningful and beneficial way.

It was many years before I understood what that actually meant. Service is not self-sacrifice. Caring is not carrying everyone.

Before I studied medicine, I studied poetry and martial arts, drawn to the ways language and movement shape experience. That curiosity led me into formal study in integrated Chinese medicine and, eventually, into clinical practice. That led to a twenty-five-year private practice, listening closely to patients living with cancer, autoimmune diseases, chronic pain, and the quieter disruptions of life, which taught me that health is not a fixed state but a gentle fluid process of noticing and rebalancing. Alongside that work, I continued a lifelong study of Qigong, Tai Chi, and Daoism, shaped by mentors who taught me stillness, presence, discipline, vision, discernment, and action.

Over time, my work expanded into working one-on-one with leaders responsible for guiding organizations and carrying the weight of constant challenges, pressures, and uncertainty. No matter the setting, whether a CEO, a leadership team, a head of state, or an artist, the practice remained the same: being still, listening deeply, observing patterns, and helping people meet complexity with clarity.

I coached leaders from the outside. I'd sit with someone, name the pattern, offer the practice, watch the shift, and check back in. It was meaningful work. I loved it (still do). But I kept thinking about how to reach beyond the individual, from empowering one person to empowering a group, a system, a culture.

In 2019, a Qigong and coaching student as well as a dear friend, Vinay Nair, invited me to lead an offsite for the leadership team at his Fin-tech startup called TIFIN. "Shake things up," he said. "I want to foster a deeper connection between all of us."

I took that to heart and guided the group through a Daoist shaking practice. The practice is always a little uncomfortable for people at first. They begin by jumping up and down together, but by the end of our practice, the result was unmistakable. The room had shifted, from awkward and self-conscious to open, grounded, and connected. Once the group was open, we could dive in deeper. Embodied practices move groups into connection very fast.

My role at TIFIN evolved from leading off-sites to coaching the leadership team and introducing embodied practices throughout the company. In 2022, I joined full-time as Chief Mindfulness Officer, bringing this work inside the organization and shaping a culture of conscious leadership, even as its full impact was still unfolding.

I spent the last four years embedded at TIFIN. Very quickly, I realized I wasn't visiting. I was in it. The pace. The pressure. The quarterly targets. The personalities. The constant sense of urgency in everything. The first six months in the company were a test of everything I knew. I reached for strategies that had served me well and watched them misfire. Not because the tools were bad, but because the terrain was different. A conversation I thought went beautifully led to little change. A new framework people were excited to implement would get displaced by urgency before it had a chance to take root.

I learned quickly that a company has an immune system. When you try to change how it operates, that system protects what it already knows. I worked person by person, giving people practical skills instead of abstract ideas: how to stay present when it mattered, how to tell hard truths in a way that opened paths forward instead of shutting people down, and how to recover after conflict instead of carrying it into the next meeting. Those small changes at the individual level didn't stay small. They moved through the company and began to shift the culture.

Another insight was the need to expand our focus beyond executives. It was easy to fixate on the top team. But we discovered that culture does not change because leaders attend workshops. Culture changes through the daily behavior of the people in the trenches. The rising leaders. The managers leading the one-on-ones, setting expectations, giving feedback, handling tension, and making decisions in real-time.

Slowly, the work began to take root. Language and practices moved through the organization like a ripple, not because anyone mandated them, but because people could feel the shift. A quiet understanding that the real work of leadership is not managing tasks or optimizing systems. It is developing the potential in other people, beginning with yourself.

What I learned through both failure and success became the material for this book.

HOW TO USE THIS BOOK

This is a book of practices to explore, test, and inhabit. It offers real tools you can use immediately, not abstract ideas to agree or disagree with.

I will not ask you to "be more mindful" or "be more authentic," nor send you back into your life with a list of inspirational quotes. You will not find concepts to memorize here. The learning happens through doing, and you will feel the difference.

These practices draw from Chinese medicine, contemplative traditions, martial arts, and neuroscience. They have been refined through decades of work with patients, students, leaders, and have been tested in real-life settings.

Each practice is an invitation. Everyone is a template meant to be adapted to your individual needs. Some will resonate. Some will not. Use what works for you.

As you develop these practices, you are not only transforming yourself. You are learning a language you share through example. The practices in this book are designed to spread, simple enough to use in a team meeting, and powerful enough to shift a culture. What begins as personal development becomes the seed of something much larger.

The ripple I saw in that church in Boston was the embodiment of presence and care: the impact of a man who showed up in moments that mattered and left behind people who were steadier because he had.

So, let's start.

"Empty yourself of everything.
Let the mind rest at peace.
The ten thousand things rise and fall
while the Self watches their return."

Dao De Jing - Lao Tzu
Translated by Gia-Fu Feng & Jane English

1

THE WAY OF LISTENING

"The sage's mind is like a mirror grasping nothing, rejecting nothing, responding without holding."
— Zhuang Zi

In the Daoist understanding of human experience, we are shaped by three energetic states: **Jing**, the physical body; **Qi**, our mental and emotional energy; and **Shen**, intuition, or the knowing beneath thought. Together, they form a framework for interpreting the raw data of the human experience. Each channel is continuously broadcasting information about our lives. Most of us rely on one channel by habit. When we learn to listen to all three, our capacity to be present deepens, and with it, our ability to respond with clarity, steadiness, and insight.

When seen this way, it becomes easier to listen to our internal landscape and to those around us. For a leader, listening with all three channels is the foundational skill, it is the tool you will return to again and again in all areas of your work. Our ability to listen can dramatically change the outcome. Listening means being present, even when we know the terrain, because change can happen fast, and we risk being blindsided if we don't adapt just as fast.

January 2, 2021, I was in Armonk, New York preparing to teach a Qigong class online. A quiet Saturday morning, ten months into the pandemic, that had forced me to close both my medical practice and our movement studio in New York City, so I was alone in the building. As I moved through my pre-class routine, an ache bloomed in my chest. *Just a muscle spasm,* I told myself, stretching and twisting to find relief. But the pressure built, and a thought surfaced that I couldn't push away: *What if this was the blow that killed my father, my grandfather, and my brother?* I was 57 years old, the same age my father was when heart disease took him.

I made my decision. No ambulance. No waiting. I did a few rounds of high-volume deep breathing to give my body all the oxygen I could, opened all my car windows to the biting winter air, asked Siri for the closest ER, and drove myself to the hospital. Walking in was my last clear memory before the gurney, the urgent voices, the monitoring equipment.

"You've had a heart attack," the doctor confirmed hours later. "But because you got here quickly, we caught it before any damage was done to your heart. We're going to put a stent in, and you'll be fine."

I had spent my adult life teaching three-channel listening: tuning into body, mind, and intuition simultaneously. My body sent signals while my rational mind was still processing, but that deeper knowing, the one down in my bones, knew exactly what to do.

This is where transformation begins: not with new information, but with learning to hear what is already being communicated.

The Three Channels

If presence is our lighthouse, then listening is our vessel. Think of each pathway as a different radio frequency, each broadcasting crucial information about your life. Most of us are tuned into only one channel at a time, missing the full range of what's available.

Jing is physical body awareness. When you feel your shoulders creep toward your ears during a difficult conversation, that's Jing speaking. When your gut tightens before a decision, that's information. The body often knows things before the conscious mind catches up. This channel communicates through sensation: tension, ease, energy, fatigue, pain, pleasure.

But how do you know if a tightening in your chest means "this is wrong for me" or "this matters so much it terrifies me?" The sensations can feel identical. The difference often reveals itself through a second layer of listening. Fear that's protecting you from genuine harm tends to feel contracting, pulling you inward and downward. Fear that's guarding a threshold you need to cross often has an electric quality underneath, a charge that feels more like excitement compressed into a small space. With practice, you learn your body's specific vocabulary.

Qi operates through your mental and emotional landscape. When the same worry loops through your mind at 3 AM, that's Qi showing you where you're stuck. When you feel suddenly irritable for no apparent reason, Qi is flagging something that needs attention. This channel reveals itself in thought patterns, emotional responses, and the quality of your attention.

Working with Qi is less like solving a problem and more like guiding water. You can't force a river to change course by pushing against it. But you can create pathways that invite the water to flow where it needs to go. When you notice a thought loop, the instinct is to fight it or figure it out. The more skillful move is to create space around it. Ask: What is this pattern protecting? What would I have to feel if this worry stopped? Often the loop is doing a job, keeping something else at bay. When you understand the job, the pattern can soften on its own.

Shen is intuitive knowing, the most subtle channel. This is the quiet voice that speaks beneath the noise of thought and sensation. It communicates through sudden clarity, through knowing without knowing how you know, and through the recognition of what's true even when it contradicts logic.

I witnessed this capacity in its most developed form in a small treatment room in Nanchang, China. It was February 2000. Late afternoon sun filtered through curtained windows, casting long shadows across the wooden floor. Stale cigarette smoke hung in the air, and I couldn't help thinking that I had traveled to the 1950s, where doctors smoked unfiltered Lucky Strikes. I had been there for about ten days, training at the Jiang Xi University Traditional Medicine Hospital.

At that time, China was in conflict with itself, pushing hard into the future of science and technology, but I had shown up looking for its past, searching for the root of this ancient medicine I had studied for seven years. My real-time translator was talking very fast, and I was trying to parse the English from the Chinese being spoken simultaneously as the doctor questioned his patient, a middle-aged woman with an autoimmune disease. The cacophony took all of my attention.

Then silence took over the room.

The elderly doctor sat across from me, his fingers resting lightly on the patient's wrist, as he studied her pulse. The room was so quiet I could hear my heartbeat and the rustle of leaves from the courtyard outside. Three minutes passed. The doctor hadn't moved, hadn't spoken. He had done nothing except pour every ounce of his attention into listening through his fingertips to the story being told by his patient's pulse.

When he finally opened his eyes and began speaking, he described not just the physical symptoms but the emotional weight the patient was carrying. The patient's eyes widened in recognition. "But how did you know?" they asked.

The doctor smiled. "When you learn to listen with your whole being, the body reveals itself."

At its deepest level, Shen listening extends beyond what the rational mind considers possible. Most of us have had experiences we can't explain:

thinking of someone moments before they call, sensing that something is wrong with a loved one at a great distance, knowing with certainty how a situation will unfold before it does. These aren't coincidences or wishful thinking. They're glimpses of what becomes consistently accessible when Shen is developed.

The night my father died, I was in San Francisco, three thousand miles from his hospital bed in New York. I woke suddenly in the dark, my heart pounding, certain that something was wrong. Moments later, the phone rang. He had suffered a massive heart attack. By the time I reached him, he was gone.

I didn't hear the phone ring from across a continent. I didn't deduce that a man with a history of heart disease might be in trouble. Something else happened, something the rational mind has no framework for. Information arrived without traveling through ordinary channels.

The ancient traditions understood consciousness as nonlocal, not confined to the body or the present moment. What quantum physics describes as superposition and the observer effect, what Otto Scharmer calls "presencing," points toward the same recognition: awareness can access information arising from the future, from distant locations, from sources the five senses cannot reach. The doctor in that treatment room wasn't performing magic. He was demonstrating a capacity we all possess, one that opens when we learn to quiet the noise of ordinary perception and listen at the level of Shen.

The power of three-channel listening comes from integration. When all three channels are accessible, you can allow the most relevant information to emerge naturally rather than forcing any single perspective to dominate.

Three-Channel Listening in Action

Last year I worked with Graham, a senior leader at a large financial technology company in New York. He's an old friend, someone who has led many companies to success by powering their sales operations. He is brilliant and analytical by nature. But when he reached out, our conversation caught me by surprise.

He opened with: "Something feels off."

He was running a division and wasn't sure where he was misaligned. He felt tired, unmotivated, and his focus was scattered. All of these feelings showed up in his body without a clear cause. He wasn't sick; his health was fine. It was confusing because he was successful, his team and boss appreciated the value he was bringing, but he felt stuck.

This is Jing listening. His body was trying to talk to him, trying to flag an issue from his unconscious that needed to be brought to the surface.

When Graham and I started talking about what he loved in his work, it became clear that he was at his peak performance when he was building teams, elevating people's skill levels, and empowering others to rise to higher levels of achievement. His joy was in coaching as well as doing. He loved to close a big deal, but he got even more pleasure in helping someone on his team do it.

Once we identified this, we realized his path forward had to incorporate coaching and development into his work. To achieve it, Graham had to step into the larger picture of how the company culture operated. He could see that the "bottom line" was the only real measure of success there, but that didn't mean there weren't ways to do both.

This is where Qi listening became essential. Graham examined the mental patterns that had been keeping him stuck. He noticed a belief running beneath the surface: that advocating for what he loved would be rejected or seen as uncommitted to results. He had internalized the company's metrics as his own measure of worth. Once he saw this pattern clearly, I asked him where his own values intersected with the company's metrics. From that vantage point, he could question them rather than be driven by them. This is how he unlocked both high performance and a sense of fulfillment.

I taught Graham a simple meditation to quiet his mind and body, allowing him to attune to his intuition. A creative solution began to emerge. He coached his team in the player-coach style he believed in and took a calculated risk, trusting that this approach would still deliver on the numbers that mattered to the company. With this new alignment, his energy, focus, and excitement returned. The team hit their numbers, morale grew, and people felt valued. Graham found a way to integrate the culture of the company with the way he loved to work. Now, when things feel off, he returns to three-channel listening to recognize misalignment earlier and keep himself on track.

The Parasympathetic Portal

Why did the elderly doctor in China sit in silence before he took the patient's pulse? Because deep listening requires a level of stillness that is achieved when our nervous system is in a relaxed state.

Our autonomic nervous system operates in two primary modes. The **sympathetic pathway** is the road of action, urgency, and response to danger. The **parasympathetic pathway** is the road of rest, renewal, and deep listening. In modern life, many of us are stuck in the sympathetic fast lane, our bodies humming with constant activation. In that state, our bodies are too "loud" to tune in to more subtle information.

Learning to access the Parasympathetic Portal is the first step in developing the art of deep listening. Our nervous system needs to be quiet for us to truly hear.

The most direct way to access this state is through breath. Slow, conscious breathing signals your system to shift from activation to reception, from loud to quiet. The body recognizes these conditions as safe enough to open and listen. We simply need to remember how to get there. When you extend your exhale longer than your inhale, you stimulate what's called vagal tone. This activates the vagus nerve, a primary driver of the parasympathetic nervous system, making it easier to settle into a quiet, receptive state. With practice, this simple technique consistently quiets the mind and body, creating the conditions to respond with greater discernment.

The skill lies in recognizing misalignment early and converting stress-driven constriction into openness and presence.

Integration Under Pressure

For leaders, the value of a quiet mind is revealed under pressure. When the stakes are high and time is scarce, integration across body, energy, and awareness determines whether a response is reactive or precise.

Captain Chesley "Sully" Sullenberger's decision to land US Airways Flight 1549 on the Hudson River provides a compelling example of all three channels working together under extreme pressure. On January 15, 2009, when both engines failed after a bird strike, Captain Sullenberger had mere minutes to make a decision that would determine the fate of 155 people.

Jing: Sullenberger described feeling the aircraft's response through his hands on the controls, sensing the unusual vibrations and the plane's altered flight characteristics. He noted his heightened physical awareness of the cockpit environment and his own bodily responses to the crisis. Rather than being overwhelmed by the stress response, he used these sensations as data.

Qi: Simultaneously, he engaged in rapid analytical processing, moving through emergency protocols, ruling out nearby airports based on altitude loss and glide distance, and recalculating options as conditions changed.

Shen: Sullenberger later described accessing what he called "a lifetime of training and experience," allowing him to synthesize information beyond conscious analysis. The decision to attempt the water landing emerged as a clear direction rather than a calculation, a form of knowing shaped by preparation and presence.

The integration of all three levels led to his decision to attempt the Hudson River landing rather than trying to reach nearby airports. Post-accident analysis confirmed that his intuitive assessment was correct: attempts to reach either airport would likely have resulted in catastrophic failure.

We may not have 155 lives in our hands, but the same capacity to integrate, clearly perceive our environment, and stay present matters in every environment where decisions are made under pressure.

Practice: Three-Channel Listening

Applied Insights

Three-Channel Listening builds your capacity to gather and integrate intelligence from your body, mind, and intuition. With practice, this allows you to navigate complexity with greater clarity and make decisions that are grounded, aligned, and measured.

When to Use

- Before making a significant decision where the "right" answer isn't obvious
- When you feel stuck or confused about a situation
- When your logical analysis keeps circling without resolution
- During or after a conversation that left you unsettled
- When you sense something is off, but you can't name it
- As a daily practice to build the skill before you need it under pressure

Method

Before you begin, take a moment to name what you're bringing to this practice. Write a clear sentence that captures the question you're holding, the decision you're facing, or the situation you need to navigate. This will be your compass, keeping you aligned to the question.

Phase One: Jing (Body)

Sit reclined or lying down. (This is a nice practice to do when you get into bed at the end of the night, or taking a rest in the afternoon.) Place your hands palm over palm, resting on your abdomen. This physical connection grounds you in the tradition of pulse diagnosis while creating a tangible entry point into body awareness.

Try to feel your heartbeat in your palms (or imagine it). Visualize your heart slowing to a relaxed speed. Now expand your attention to scan your entire body in relation to your chosen situation. Notice where tension emerges when you think about this challenge.

These physical responses are your Jing listening channel communicating what it knows. The body often recognizes misalignment before the mind can process it. Stay with this for at least one minute, simply gathering information through careful observation.

Remember the most important aspect of this practice is to build the sensitivity of listening to your body. What matters most is that you hear the alert from your body and you inquire more deeply.

Phase Two: Qi (Mind and Emotion)

Maintaining light contact with your hands resting in your lap, shift your attention to the mental and emotional patterns that arise around your situation. Rather than following individual thoughts, notice the patterns themselves.

Does your mind loop through the same concerns repeatedly? Does it avoid certain aspects? Does it jump to worst-case scenarios or inflate best-case outcomes?

Notice whether certain thoughts connect to physical sensations. This cross-referencing begins to map the interconnection between your thoughts and your body around this challenge. Observe your thoughts and physical sensations without trying to solve the issue. You're simply paying attention to how you are processing. When it feels clear, make a mental note of the landscape. For example, when I'm thinking about this situation, I feel sluggish in my body, my energy drops, and my mind gets stuck in the same ineffective answer over and over.

Phase Three: Shen (Intuition)

Now allow your focus to soften. Release the effort to actively gather information and instead create space for deeper knowing to emerge. This may feel like looking through water, aware of what's moving below the surface without trying to name it.

The Shen channel communicates through sudden, quiet knowing, images that carry meaning, and sensations that go beyond emotion. You might notice a metaphor arising spontaneously, a memory surfacing with unexpected relevance, or a quiet certainty about what needs attention.

Sometimes Shen communicates through absence: what you stop thinking about, or what your body suddenly releases.

You may also receive information whose relevance isn't immediately clear. These often arrive as answers to questions you haven't yet asked, or insights whose application only becomes apparent over time.

For example, you may be considering a change in your role and suddenly picture a highway. The image makes no sense in the moment. Later, you realize the right opportunity required relocation. It's not magic, it's access to more information than we typically use, broadening the potential for understanding.

Integration

After moving through all three channels, take some time to synthesize by writing your thoughts in your journal. What does your body know that your mind is avoiding? What does your intuition sense that your emotions are obscuring? What is the solution or path where the information in all three channels aligns?

Adaptations

Two-Minute Version: Skip the pulse contact. Simply ask three questions in sequence: What is my body telling me? What patterns is my mind running? What do I know without knowing how I know it? Even this abbreviated check-in interrupts single-channel dominance.

Twenty-Minute Deep Dive: Extend each phase to five minutes. Journal what emerges from each channel before moving to the next. Use the final five minutes to look for connections and contradictions across all three.

Walking Version: Practice while walking slowly. Let your footsteps set the rhythm. Spend one-third of your walk attending to body sensations, one-third noticing thought patterns, one-third softening into intuitive awareness.

In-Conversation Use: While listening to someone speak, lightly scan all three channels. What is your body responding to? What mental judgments are forming? What intuitive read are you getting? This transforms listening from passive reception to active intelligence gathering.

Pre-Decision Ritual: Before any significant decision, pause and move through all three channels regarding each option. Create three columns (one per channel) and note what each reveals about each choice.

What to Expect

First few times: The channels may feel artificial or forced. You might struggle to distinguish body sensation from emotion, or thought from intuition. This is normal. Most people find one channel much easier to access than the others. Start there and let the others develop.

After a week of daily practice: You'll begin noticing channel-specific information spontaneously throughout your day. Your body will "speak up" during meetings. You'll catch mental loops earlier. Brief intuitive flashes will register instead of being dismissed.

After a month: The three channels start functioning as an integrated system rather than separate skills. You'll find yourself naturally cross-referencing: "My body is tense but my intuition says yes—what is my body protecting me from?" The practice becomes less about the formal structure and more about a way of being present to your full experience.

Common Obstacles

"I can't feel anything in my body." Start smaller. Can you feel your feet on the floor? Your hands in your lap? The temperature of the air? Body awareness develops through patient attention to what's actually available, not by forcing sensation to appear. If numbness is present, that itself is information worth noting.

"My mind won't stop analyzing long enough for intuition." This is the most common obstacle. Don't fight the analysis—observe it. Notice the pattern of thoughts rather than their content. When you shift from thinking *about* something to noticing *that* you're thinking, you've already begun accessing a different channel. Intuition often arrives in the gap after you've exhausted analysis, so let the mind run until it tires.

"I don't trust what I'm getting." You're not being asked to act on everything that emerges. You're learning to receive information from multiple sources. Trust develops through tracking: note what each channel told you, then observe what actually unfolds. Over time, you'll learn which signals are reliable and which are noise.

"All three channels are telling me different things." This is valuable data, not a problem. Contradictions between channels often reveal the crux of a dilemma. Your body says no, your mind says yes, your intuition says wait—now you know what needs further exploration. The goal isn't unanimous agreement but fuller awareness of what's actually present.

Field Note

Blair came into my office the morning before a critical meeting. An overseas client, one essential to the company's success, had experienced a product delivery issue. The demo hadn't performed as expected, and doubt was creeping in. She was about to face the client's leadership team, who had flown in from Australia, in person. This meeting was the opportunity to convince them that her company was the right choice.

I had her sit down and slow her breathing, extending the length of each exhale until she reached a count of eight. Within minutes, she was able to feel where her body was holding the stress: her abdomen was tight, as though she was bracing for impact.

"What's the fear?" I asked.

"That they won't close the deal. That they've lost faith in us."

I asked her to look beneath the fear to the older story. What was the emotion connected to that thought?

"That we're not good enough."

"Go a little deeper," I said.

"That I'm not enough," she finally said with a big sigh.

As soon as she said it out loud, we could see it for what it was. We broke it down. Were there facts to support that belief? She had earned her role through demonstrated capability and track record. The story sounded like an old pattern, but it held no truth for her anymore. Naming it loosened its grip, allowing her to release the pattern with some big exhales.

The next question: "How do you achieve your goal of having them trust you?"

She sat with it, her body now relaxed and her mind quiet. After about a minute, she looked up. "I have to show up as myself, without filter or reservation. When I try to be something extra, when I defend or prove, it doesn't work. All I have to do is be who I am."

That afternoon, she found me to share what happened. She had walked into the meeting without the armor of proving something, centered in who she was and what she brought to the table. The client's concerns dissolved. But more than the outcome, what stayed with her was the recognition that the preparation that mattered most wasn't rehearsing her talking points. It was clearing what was in the way of her showing up as her complete, authentic self.

Blair was able to activate her Jing listening and hear her body's signal. When she released the tension she was holding, she used Qi listening to unlock the story she was telling herself. Lastly, she stepped into Shen listening by paying attention to the voice of her true self.

Remember This

Deep listening is the foundation upon which all transformation builds. Before we can change anything, we must first learn to hear what is already being communicated.

Jing attunes us to the wisdom of the body. Qi reveals the patterns of thought and emotion. Shen opens us to intuitive knowing that transcends ordinary perception. These aren't separate skills to master, but different frequencies already operating within you. The practice is removing what blocks your access to them.

Integration creates clarity that no single channel can provide. Like Sullenberger reading multiple streams of information in those critical moments over the Hudson, you can learn to gather intelligence from body, mind, and intuition at once.

Deep listening requires a quiet nervous system. The Parasympathetic Portal, accessed through slow breathing with extended exhales, creates the conditions where subtle signals can finally be heard.

2

BREAKING THE PATTERN

"Be patient toward all that is unsolved in your heart and try to love the questions themselves."
— Rainer Maria Rilke

I was on the side of a mountain in Colorado. I had two gallons of water and a sleeping bag. Three days alone. No phone. No distractions. Just me and the wilderness.

As a city kid from Boston, my experience with nature had been limited. I spent my youth skateboarding through concrete canyons rather than natural ones. So, when my teacher suggested a solo wilderness quest, I approached it with the enthusiasm of someone who had no idea what he was getting into.

"This is going to be amazing!" I thought, on the first day. "I'm going to grow and expand in so many ways." I had expectations of immediate transformation. Lightning bolts of insight. Visions that would reshape my understanding of everything.

The mountain's response was silence.

As night fell and I found myself without phone or distractions, anxiety crept in. I spent that first night waiting for some dramatic spiritual experience, shouting at the sky: "When does the lightning bolt strike and I get enlightened with new wisdom?"

Nothing happened.

Through the first twenty-four hours, as my body and mind began to slowly grow quiet I started to hear something different. Not the revelations I had demanded, but the mountain's own stories. The story of a great mother who sheltered creatures from harsh winds. How she provided hunting grounds for young animals learning to thrive. The mountain's stillness began to grow within me, teaching me to create a quiet spaciousness for something new to emerge.

On the final night, while watching the stars through a circular opening in the tree canopy, something subtle shifted. It felt like a rope I hadn't known was there suddenly loosened from around my heart. As I lay on a cool stone ledge, memories from childhood began to surface. But these weren't the traumatic ones I'd focused on for years. Instead, I remembered moments of joy and connection with my parents. My father teaching me to make bread. My mother walking with me to the coffee shop, laughing together about school stories. These memories carried a deep sense of the love they'd always had for me, though both had been dead for twenty years by then.

This experience revealed something I had understood intellectually but never felt in my body: my perception had been fractured. For years, I had focused on pain and missed the fuller truth of my relationship with my parents. The gratitude that flooded through me that night worked like a psychological editor, clearing away old grooves of anger, grief, and judgment, rewriting them with understanding, gratitude, and empathy.

I came down from that mountain different than I went up. Not because of lightning bolts or mystical visions, but because my system had relaxed long enough for a deeper, more complete awareness to emerge.

The Hardware We're Built With

For years afterward, I wrestled with a question that experience had surfaced. Why can we understand intellectually that everything is connected, that we're all part of one interdependent system, but we can't actually feel it or experience it directly?

We can see scientifically that at the atomic level; we are in energetic exchange with everything all the time. Yet we "visit" nature instead of just "being nature." It would be like a grain of sand saying it wants to go to the beach to "experience" the sand. It seems absurd.

More than absurd, this sense of separation appears to be the root cause of so much conflict and suffering. If we could truly feel our interconnection to each other, it would reduce human suffering and create unprecedented growth in our collective evolution. True empathy lives in this understanding. When we sense our interconnection, strangers stop being "other." They become recognizable as part of our extended family. Not in some abstract philosophical sense, but in the immediate felt recognition that we share the same fundamental nature.

Eventually, I realized this separation isn't a defect in our design. It's a feature.

We experience separation because our brains need filters to function. If we truly felt our connection to everything all the time, we'd be completely overwhelmed. Imagine trying to make any decision while simultaneously processing your connection to every person, every ecosystem, and every consequence rippling outward. You'd be paralyzed by too much information. Our sense of separation lets us navigate daily life without drowning in complexity.

But here's what makes this interesting: even though we need these filters to function, our sense of right and wrong, compassion, love, all of our most important values, come from this deeper knowing that we're all connected. We're wired to experience life as individuals, while our moral compass points toward the truth of our deeper unity.

This is why practices that temporarily relax our filters matter so much.

The wilderness solo didn't give me new information. It quieted my habitual filtering long enough for information that was always there to finally reach me. The memories of my parents' love hadn't disappeared. My perceptual system had simply been screening them out, letting through only what confirmed my existing story about my childhood.

We need our filters. We also need practices that help us see beyond them. Both are true.

The Prediction Engine

Think about how your mind processes the world around you. Your perception resembles an intricate tapestry, woven from countless threads of experiences and memories. Each thread represents a lesson learned, a habit recognized, a prediction about how the world works.

When you walk into a kitchen filled with the smells of your favorite childhood meal, your body responds automatically. Your mouth waters, your stomach rumbles, and memories of family surface unbidden. This automatic response demonstrates how deeply our experiences shape our reality and influence our expectations.

The power and limitation of our predictive mind lies in its efficiency. We've become so adept at categorizing and responding to our environment that we often miss the infinite possibilities available in the present.

I learned this growing up with an alcoholic father in Boston. I developed a state of hypervigilance around him. I could tell by his gait, the micro-expressions in his face, and the tone of his voice whether it was going to be safe or not. I would predict his behavior, and this ability kept me safe in an environment that wasn't.

At the time, it served my survival. Later, it got in the way.

As an adult, every time I entered a bar, I'd see people drinking and having fun, but my mind would recognize the pattern as danger. My nervous system would prepare for conflict. For a long time, I didn't even realize I was doing it. I just felt uncomfortable in bars. My body would tense. I'd watch people's movements with suspicion. The filtering system that had protected me as a child was now distorting my perception as an adult.

When my practice evolved and my self-awareness increased, I realized what was happening. This awareness led to one of my earliest experiments in recalibration.

My wife was a musician and was very comfortable in bars. I would bring her with me, and we would observe people who were drinking and having fun. I'd ask her to help me assess whether this person was actually dangerous or simply relaxed. Over time, I developed a new set of parameters for perceiving drinking in a bar. Gradually I rewrote my brain's automatic responses and began to feel clear in those environments.

This process taught me how deeply our early experiences shape our perception. We carry these formative moments unconsciously into our adult lives, regularly narrowing our perception in ways that ultimately don't serve us. But we can consciously transform these habits through recalibration and clear observation.

Our minds excel at pattern recognition, creating deep grooves of expectation. These grooves can serve us well, like anticipating a delicious meal when we smell cooking. They can also trap us in limiting beliefs and cause us to miss opportunities right in front of us.

The antidote is to maintain presence, noticing the world as a changing system rather than a fixed picture. Stay open to possibilities as they arise.

Nature as Pattern Breaker

Tools for expanding our perception and softening those deep habitual grooves are essential for seeing the world more clearly. Wisdom traditions have long offered such tools. As we saw in Chapter 1, practices like the body scan help you notice sensation changes that are early indicators of stress. Practices that allow you to observe your thoughts before your conscious mind latches onto them generate more accurate observations of the present moment. Changing where you place your attention shifts your perception to new information.

The natural world offers perhaps the most effective way to reset our perception. Nature, with its unspoken wisdom and tranquil presence, provides an ideal setting for healing our fractured relationship with reality. A forest, mountain, or desert landscape offers a sanctuary where the essence of your being becomes visible against the backdrop of the natural world.

The simplicity of nature strips away our usual distractions and allows us to see ourselves more clearly.

In a 2019 study published in Frontiers in Psychology, researchers documented that just twenty minutes of nature contact significantly lowered stress hormone levels. EEG measurements showed increased alpha wave activity, indicating relaxed alertness and enhanced creative thinking. But we don't need a study to tell us that walking barefoot on summer grass gives an immediate sense of grounding and presence.

When we step away from digital devices and immerse ourselves in the natural world, a transformation begins. Our minds expand. Our senses sharpen. Study participants who spent time in natural settings before tackling complex problems demonstrated improved executive attention, working memory, and cognitive flexibility.

The Three Views

That experience on the mountain taught me something I've used ever since. When facing any situation, especially one where you feel stuck or reactive, practice viewing it through three distinct lenses:

Personal View: Notice your immediate reaction and the assumptions behind it. What past experiences might be coloring your perception? This is where I started when I noticed my discomfort in bars. I had to recognize that my reaction belonged to my history, not necessarily to the present moment.

Observer View: Step back and observe the situation as if watching a scene in a movie. What details might you be missing from your personal viewpoint? This is what my wife helped me do. She could see what I couldn't because she wasn't filtering through my childhood experience.

Ecosystem View: Expand your awareness to see the interconnections at play. Think about how a forest functions: the trees, the soil, the insects, the weather, the decay, and regeneration all operating together. No single element makes sense in isolation. When you see the whole system with all its relationships and cycles, you understand what any individual part truly is and how it will behave. Apply this same lens to your situation. How does it fit into larger patterns and relationships? A bar is part of a neighborhood, a culture, a human tradition of gathering. Seeing the larger context changes what any individual moment means.

By deliberately shifting between these perspectives, you create space between stimulus and response. This practice changes how you see. It transforms things from hidden to visible.

Practice: The Perception Reset

Applied Insights

This practice builds your capacity to break free from habitual patterns that limit how you see situations, people, and possibilities. This practice uses nature's elegant complexity to hold you while disrupting your mind's predictive frameworks, revealing the constructed narrative of your experience. Over time, this awareness will give you the ability to shift perceptual modes fluidly, seeing what was previously hidden.

When to Use

- When your thinking produces the same unsatisfactory conclusions
- When a situation feels stuck or unchangeable
- When you notice repetitive mental loops about a challenge
- When strategic planning feels constrained by limited options
- When a relationship dynamic seems fixed and unworkable
- Before making important decisions where fresh perspective would help

The Practice

Find 10—30 minutes and a natural setting with some complexity: a park, garden, or even a single tree.

Phase One: Pattern Recognition

Before engaging with nature, articulate your current perception of your chosen situation. Write how you see the problem and what feels unchangeable. This establishes your baseline perceptual groove and allows you to begin mapping any habitual narrative.

Now engage with the natural environment using your habitual way of seeing. If you're analytical, start categorizing what you observe. If you're emotional, notice your feelings about the environment. Don't try to change this. Simply notice how your consciousness immediately organizes the natural world according to existing patterns and creates stories based on expectation rather than neutral observation.

Phase Two: The Perception Shift

Deliberately shift from your habitual way of engaging, whether active analysis or emotional engagement, etc. Move into a state of receptive awareness by allowing the natural environment to reach toward you rather than you reaching out to understand it. Let your vision soften and pay attention to all your senses, so you're taking in the whole, rather than focusing on parts.

Notice what you started to experience: spaces between leaves, quality of shadows, movements too slow for normal attention, sounds and textures coming through. This reveals how much your predictive patterns filter out. Stay in this receptive state until you feel your perceptual framework loosening and opening. There is often a greater relaxation that you will start to notice as this part of the practice stabilizes.

Phase Three: Three-View Integration

Apply the Three Views framework to both the natural environment and your situation:

Personal View: Notice a specific natural element and observe how your mind creates meaning around it. Then examine your situation through this same awareness. What stories are you telling that might not be true?

Observer View: Step back into a witnessing perspective, seeing yourself as part of the landscape. From this position, observe your situation as if watching someone else navigate it. What becomes visible from this removed perspective?

Ecosystem View: Expand awareness to perceive interconnections at a larger scale. See how the tree connects to soil, air, water, insects, birds, and weather. Notice how decay feeds new growth, how competition and cooperation exist simultaneously. Now view your situation within its larger ecosystem. What relationships have you been missing? What cycles are operating that you haven't noticed?

Integration

After moving through all three views, return to your situation through the lens of this natural intelligence. Ask: If your challenge was occurring in nature, how would natural systems respond? How would nature adapt gradually, rather than seeking immediate transformation? How would it create cooperative or competitive relationships to accommodate this new information?

Write this new perception without reverting to your original framework. Describe your situation as a natural phenomenon rather than a human problem. A "competitive threat" might become "an adjacent system seeking similar resources." An "impossible deadline" might become "a seasonal cycle requiring different responses."

Document both your original perception and this nature-informed view. The contrast reveals not just new solutions but different ways of understanding the situation itself.

Adaptations

Quick version (5 minutes): Step outside or look out a window. Name your stuck situation in one sentence. Take three breaths while gazing at something natural. Ask: "What am I not seeing?" Let your vision soften. Notice what shifts in how you're holding the problem.

Deep version (30 minutes): Take a nature walk with your situation in mind. Spend extended time in each of the three views. Journal between phases. End by sitting quietly and letting new perception consolidate before returning to regular activity.

Urban version: Use any living thing: a houseplant, a pigeon, a patch of weeds in sidewalk cracks. The principle holds. Nature disrupts human frameworks wherever it appears. Even watching clouds or feeling the wind works.

Meeting prep: Before a difficult conversation or strategic session, spend five minutes with the ecosystem view. Ask: "What's the larger system this situation sits within? What relationships and cycles am I missing?" Enter the meeting with peripheral vision engaged.

Evening reflection: At day's end, briefly revisit a challenge through the three views. Notice how your perception has shifted since morning. This builds the habit of multiple-perspective seeing.

What to Expect

First few times: You may find it difficult to shift out of analytical mode. The instruction to let nature "reach toward you" might feel abstract. Your mind will want to categorize and understand rather than simply receive. The three views may feel like a mental exercise rather than a genuine perceptual shift. This is normal. Start with whichever view comes most naturally and let the others develop.

After one week of practice: You'll start noticing your perceptual habits in real-time, catching yourself mid-assumption. The three views become easier to access, and you may find yourself spontaneously softening your vision during the day. Your stuck situations begin to feel less solid.

After one month: The practice becomes a reliable pattern interruption tool you can deploy quickly. You'll develop a felt sense for when your perception has narrowed and needs resetting. The ecosystem view in particular begins to inform how you see challenges without requiring formal practice.

Common Obstacles

"I can't get to nature." You don't need wilderness. A single plant, a view of sky, moving water, even photographs of nature can trigger the perceptual shift. The key is engaging with something that doesn't conform to human mental frameworks.

"My mind keeps returning to problem-solving mode." This is the pattern asserting itself. When you notice this, gently return to receptive awareness. Each return is the practice working. The mind's grip loosens incrementally.

"The new perception doesn't feel as 'true' as my original view." Of course it doesn't. You've rehearsed your original perception thousands of times. The new view is unfamiliar, not wrong. Hold both perspectives lightly. See which proves more useful over time.

"I don't have 30 minutes." Use the quick version consistently rather than waiting for ideal conditions. Five minutes of genuine perception shift beats thirty minutes of frustrated striving.

Field Note

Maya, one of the cofounders of a nonprofit I was working with, had been stuck for months in a frustrating dynamic with her cofounder. She never felt like she was doing enough. Her cofounder seemed to always be doing more and complained about it. Yet when Maya looked at her cofounder's work, it didn't seem effective. Both were exhausted. Neither felt appreciated. Every conversation about workload turned into quiet resentment.

One afternoon, she went to a local park to do the practice. She found a bench facing a large oak and let her vision soften. As she sat with the tree, she noticed a nest tucked into one of the upper branches. The tree wasn't just producing oxygen or providing shade. It was also a shelter, a home. Multiple functions, one organism.

Something shifted. She realized she had been seeing the partnership from only one angle, and that angle was filled with assumptions about roles and contributions. When she widened to the ecosystem view, the question changed. Instead of "what am I doing?" and "what is she doing?" it became "what does the organization need to be healthy?"

The situation hadn't changed. But the false conflict her mind had constructed dissolved into a more useful question: what could they do together that would serve the mission best? When she brought that question to her next conversation with her cofounder, they stopped comparing workloads and started redesigning how they divided responsibilities based on what the organization actually needed.

Remember This

The wisdom we seek isn't only found in accumulating more knowledge or achieving more goals. It also lives in remembering our place in the great web of life; in healing the artificial separations we've created between each other and the world.

We experience separation because our brains need filters to function. This is hardware, not defect. Yet our deepest values arise from our underlying connection to everything. We're wired to operate as individuals while our moral compass points toward unity. Both are true. This is why practices that temporarily relax our filtering matter so much.

Our minds excel at pattern recognition, creating deep grooves of expectation that help us navigate familiar territory. These habits can serve us well, and they can also trap us in limiting beliefs. The patterns that protected you in one phase of life may distort your perception in another. Conscious recalibration is always possible.

Nature offers the most effective way to reset our perception because it refuses to conform to our mental frameworks. In each moment of genuine contact with the natural world lies an opportunity to remember our true nature, to heal the fractures in our perception, and to see with greater clarity.

3

LET GO

"The softest thing in the world
overcomes the hardest thing in the world."
— Lao Tzu

Surrender is a word filled with so many layers of meaning. It can evoke ideas of compromising, giving up, losing, or even a doorway to healing as in the "serenity prayer" shared in 12 Step groups. But let's set aside the conventional notions and look through a particular lens at what it means to surrender consciously and how that affects the way we move through our lives.

First, let's look at the opposite of surrender. Whether you call it attachment, judgment, determination, drive, or goals, we are talking about being focused on the expectation of the result you have in your mind. This is how we all get things done. It's how we build everything from our careers to bridges and highways, and it works great, right up until the moment it doesn't.

The critical moment, when we need to pay attention, is when we realize that we're at a point where we're not going to get the result we thought we wanted. At this moment, we come to a crossroads. In one direction lies the willingness to adapt, shift our expectations, and pivot. In the other direction lies white-knuckling it and trying to force the result even though it has become misaligned.

In order to even be able to take action, we have to be able to notice that we're coming up to the crossroads. There aren't any stoplights at this intersection, and people often just blow right through it. The specifics are different in every situation, but it always resembles something that feels like: In baseball, there are two outs and two strikes, and success or failure is riding on how you handle the next pitch. In business, the crossroads might look like a financial runway coming to an end and the need for new investment. In your personal life, it could look like a moment where you need to either commit more deeply into a relationship or step away from it. When we come to these crossroads, it's important that we slow down, listen, and take in the situation.

Unfortunately, slowing down is often counterintuitive in these moments. It's like steering into a skid when your car loses traction. The desire to counter-steer and try to stay on course is so strong that people reflexively turn away from the skid and lose control of the car. If you turn into the skid, you will find your way back on course. This natural response, to tighten our grip when we should be loosening it, or to lean in when we want to run away, is deeply ingrained in our survival instincts. The question you need to ask isn't what you want, but what you're willing to let go of to get it.

What we have to let go of usually isn't easy. It's rooted in attachment. Otherwise, we would have dropped it a long time ago without even thinking about it. So, remember, if you're trying to figure out how to let go of something, ask yourself: Where is my attachment?

Surrender, like any skillful action, requires exquisite timing and clear discernment. Sometimes what feels like an invitation to let go is actually a test of perseverance, while what seems like a moment to persist might be life asking us to release our grip. Understanding this dance between persistence and surrender is crucial for navigating life's crossroads moments with wisdom. Ask these two questions: What am I attached to? Am I focused on what truly matters?

Surrender Isn't Giving Up

When the pandemic shuttered businesses across New York in 2020, like many people, I faced a crossroads that tested my surrender skills. After building my medical practice and The Pathfinder studio over decades, I watched as everything I had created was suddenly forced to dissolve. My immediate response was predictable: constriction, fear, and a cascade of unanswerable questions. How would I support my family? What would happen to the patients who depended on me? Would I be able to come back from this?

Like many of us, this wasn't a choice I got to make. It was thrust upon me with no room for negotiation. Unlike the calculated risks we often face in life, where we can weigh options and choose our timing, this was surrender in its most fundamental form. This was a rare and almost universal moment for so many people, where there was no way around the problem. The only way was through.

What emerged from stepping into the stillness of that forced letting go was something I could never have anticipated. For the first time since my children were born, I found myself fully present in their daily lives. Years of early morning departures and late evening returns had created a pattern I hadn't even recognized as loss until it was suddenly reversed. Now I was cooking breakfast, hearing about their school experiences in real-time, and participating in the thousand small moments that weave a family together.

This unexpected gift revealed a nuance of surrender that I had understood intellectually but never fully embodied: sometimes what we cling to so tightly prevents us from receiving what we actually need. My attachment to maintaining my practice in its traditional form had blinded me to other possibilities, both in my family life and professionally.

The second revelation came through the rapid digital transformation that the pandemic created. Teaching Qigong to an empty room while students joined from locations around the globe initially felt like a pale substitute for in-person connection. Yet as weeks turned to months, I began receiving messages from students in remote locations. A traveler quarantined in Italy. A healthcare worker finding moments of peace between shifts. A parent practicing Qigong between Zoom calls.

The constraint that had seemed so limiting had actually expanded my work's reach across the globe. The belief I had been holding onto, that authentic teaching required physical presence, was actually limiting my impact. By surrendering this attachment, I discovered that the essence of the Qigong practice could transcend physical boundaries in ways I had never imagined. Over time, I started to feel into a new level of sensing the students through the digital framework. It was amazing to actually realize we could connect so deeply through the web. It became in many ways an intimate experience of sharing and discovery.

This experience spotlighted the paradox at the heart of conscious surrender: the moment we release our attachment to things being the "right" way, we create space for possibilities we couldn't previously imagine. Like water finding its way around an immovable boulder, surrender doesn't mean giving up on our destination. It means discovering new pathways we never would have found.

This is where humility enters the equation. When we're gripping tight at a crossroads, we're usually attached to being right. Right about the outcome, right about the method, right about how things should go. Letting go requires recognizing that our way might not be the only way, or even the best way.

To paraphrase Rick Warren, author of *A Purpose Driven Life,* Humility isn't about thinking less of yourself. It's about thinking more of someone else. At the crossroads, that "someone else" might be a colleague with a different perspective, a situation that's asking for something new, or simply the possibility you haven't considered yet. A friend of mine used to say, "It's hard to be humble because it's often humiliating." What he meant was that releasing our attachment to being right can feel like not being seen for your value. It forces us to let go of our ego's desire for recognition. But that release is exactly what creates space for something better to emerge. Imagine how much time we would save if people didn't feel like they had to repeat the same thing in a meeting that someone else just said, but in different words, to show that they also knew it.

The Body Knows First

Surrender happens in the body and the mind, and our bodies are often the early warning system that helps our unconscious bring forward something that we can't put off looking at any longer. Oftentimes, when we are overrun with fight-or-flight stress and attached deeply to the result we're looking for, our minds aren't able to break through the thought patterns of attachment. But if you're able to see the attachment, you can listen to your body and begin to unlock the door to surrender and open up to new possibilities. You just need to recognize the crossroads moment and listen to your body's message. Remember, your body knows before your mind when you are holding on too tight. These physical signals are your first indicators that you need to loosen your grip and check in.

Mentally, this moment will often manifest in asking the same question over and over and arriving at the same answer. When you change the question, you release the attachment.

When you notice these warning signs, take some time to pause. This doesn't mean you need to stop everything you're doing, but that you need to create some space for your inner observer to recognize what's happening. The ability to notice a warning sign of misalignment, pause in the moment and observe your thoughts, gives you the opportunity to check in and see through the habitual behavior into the present moment. Then the questions emerge to help you find your path.

Skillful Inquiry

Once you are able to neutralize the early warning signs by relaxing your body, breathing more slowly and deeply, and letting go of looping thoughts, you can step into questions that will help you identify the root cause of the misalignment.

Start with control: Am I trying to force something that isn't actually mine to control? Most of our suffering at crossroads comes from gripping what we cannot hold. Name what's beyond your control and let that part go.

Then look for what you're missing: What solutions am I not seeing because I'm locked in my current frame? This is where the Three Views from the previous chapter become useful. Your Personal View shows your assumptions. The Observer View shows what you'd notice if this were happening to someone else. The Ecosystem View reveals the larger patterns and relationships you might be ignoring.

Finally, check alignment: Have I drifted from my values? And who do I trust, who might see what I can't? Often the path forward becomes clear when we stop asking "What should I do?" and start asking "Who am I, and what does that person do?"

Once you've identified where you're holding on and asked these questions, bring your attention fully to the present moment. What's actually happening right now, separate from your expectations or fears about outcomes? Often, when you truly see the present moment clearly, you discover that your attachment was skewed by assumptions rather than the actual facts of the moment.

Remember the crossroads metaphor. You always have choices, even if they're not the ones you originally planned for. The practice of surrender is about developing the capacity to see these choices clearly and choose wisely, rather than being driven by fear or rigid attachment to a particular outcome.

Connected Relaxation

In Tai Chi, the quality we're reaching for is called Feng Sung, which means connected relaxation. It's the art of softening tension without collapsing entirely. You're not going limp. You're not giving up. You're releasing the grip while maintaining your direction.

This is what distinguishes surrender from defeat. Defeat is collapse. Surrender is opening. When you find Feng Sung, you can take in new information and adjust your route without abandoning your destination. You stay responsive instead of rigid, fluid instead of frozen.

The practice that follows trains this capacity.

Hearing the Call

When we start using this skill and combine it with deeper listening and nature's wisdom from the chapters that came before, we gain entry into a more subtle skillful inquiry. As we get better and better at this practice over time, it starts to allow us to connect with information before it even becomes an issue. Leaders who often seem prescient and able to see around corners are usually skilled in their ability to tune in and listen and let go of a single path mindset. Then, using skillful inquiry, they can see a multitude of paths presenting themselves in the present, waiting for us to pick the future that will emerge from them.

I had this experience when my mother was sick with cancer. She had been diagnosed for about a year, and her prognosis wasn't good. I was working very hard in medical school at the time and apprenticing at a clinic.

My mom and I were really close. She was that person who had always been there for me whenever I needed someone, and I was the one she called when she wanted to share a new discovery she had encountered, or some passion she had stepped into. That year, I had made a plan to see her at the end of the semester in late May, and she had assured me she was doing fine. So, I was going to continue my studies and work and planned to see her in May.

In early April, she called me out of the blue. I thought it was just to chat. We talked for a while about everything, and then, very gently, toward the end of the conversation she said to me, "If you want to come earlier, you're welcome to." I said, "Ok, thanks. I'll think about it and let you know."

At the time, I had been reading Elizabeth Kubler-Ross's last book, The Wheel of Life: A Memoir of Living and Dying. Kubler-Ross devoted her life to studying death and dying, helping people navigate the end of life with greater awareness and less fear. It's a beautiful memoir of her life. There was a chapter in the book named "Hearing the Call." In that chapter, Kubler-Ross talks about her mother very quietly asking her to do something which later turned out to be a signal that she was going to die, and Kubler-Ross had always regretted the fact that she didn't hear the call from her mother.

As I read that chapter, I thought about my mother calling me and very gently suggesting that I come earlier, and I realized that that might be the moment that Kubler-Ross was talking about. So I booked a plane ticket the next day and flew out to Florida to see my mother. We had a full day together, and the next day her health took a serious turn. Within five days, she was gone.

The ability to let go and listen, take in all of the information emerging in the present moment, and choose the outcome most aligned with our path is the challenge that lies before us—and it's what becomes possible when we let go of attachment. It was a simple thing to slow down and listen at that moment. But such moments go by so quickly. With practice, it will become an intuition that you hone through Shen listening. Pause, enter into the present moment, and listen with your body, mind, and intuition.

If my mother hadn't died, we still would have had a lovely visit, and going early would have cost me nothing. But if I hadn't gone, I know I would have always regretted not being with my mother in those final days. Being able to hold her hand and walk her across the threshold into the next life was a gift I will never forget.

Practice: Letting Go

Applied Insights

The capacity to recognize when you're at a crossroads and make a conscious choice about whether to grip tighter or release. This practice trains you to read your body's early warning signals, distinguish between productive persistence and counterproductive attachment, and find what the Tai Chi tradition calls Feng Sung, connected relaxation that yields without collapsing.

When to Use

- When your body signals tension, shallow breathing, or bracing around a situation
- When the same thought keeps looping without resolution
- When effort is increasing but results are diminishing
- When you sense you're at a crossroads but can't see clearly
- When you're unsure whether to lean in harder or step back
- When you feel the urge to force an outcome

The Practice

Find 10-20 minutes of quiet space. This practice works best when you can move between sitting and standing. Before you begin, identify the situation where you feel stuck or are gripping too tightly. Name it clearly in your mind or write it down. This might be a decision you keep circling, a relationship dynamic that won't resolve, or an outcome you're trying to force.

Hold this situation lightly as you move through the practice. You're not here to solve it yet, you're here to understand your relationship to it.

Phase One: Body Check and Release

Stand with your spine naturally upright. Close your eyes and bring the stuck situation to mind without trying to solve it.

Notice immediately: Where does your body respond? Jaw, shoulders, chest, gut, hands? Is your breathing shallow or held? Don't analyze it yet. Just locate where the grip lives.

Now release some of that holding. Take a full breath in, sip in a little more air at the top, then let it go with an audible sigh. Do this five times. Let each exhale carry out some of the tension you noticed.

Now take a deep breath in and as you exhale let your body fold forward from your hips, letting your head and arms hang heavy and loose. Stay for two breaths. Then slowly roll back up to standing. Repeat this three times.

Maintaining this softer, more connected, and open state, step into the next phase.

Phase Two: The Crossroads Question

Ask yourself: Am I at a crossroads with this situation?

A crossroads moment is when continuing your current approach will no longer get you where you want to go. The old way keeps producing the same result. Something needs to shift, but the direction isn't clear.

If you're not at a crossroads, if this is simply a difficult stretch requiring continued effort, the practice might be recommitment rather than letting go.

Phase Three: Naming the Attachment

Ask: What am I actually attached to here? (Note: it's usually a judgment that's often rooted in childhood development)

We grip because something feels essential to protect: Whether being right or good, a specific outcome, others' perception of us, our identity, avoiding discomfort, maintaining control.

If the answer doesn't come, return to where you felt residual tension in Phase One. Ask that part of your body directly: *What are you protecting?* Let the body answer before your mind edits.

Name the attachment simply. One sentence. No justification is needed.

Phase Four: The Diagnostic

Assess honestly whether this is a moment to release or stay the course.

Signs pointing toward letting go:

- Diminishing returns despite increased effort
- Exhaustion that doesn't improve with rest
- Loss of connection to your original purpose or values

- Recurring feedback you've been dismissing
- Persistent intuitive signals that something's off

Signs pointing toward staying the course:

- Clear progress, even if slower than expected
- Challenges that strengthen rather than deplete you
- Strong alignment with core values and purpose
- Intuitive sense of rightness despite difficulty
- Resources and support still available
- Which list resonates? Let your body respond. Notice when you feel expansion and when you feel contraction.

Phase Five: Taking Action

Based on your diagnostic, choose your path.

If letting go: Stand again. Spend a few minutes focused on your breath with an extended exhale. With each exhale feel the area where tension is loosening and opening. Ask: *What's possible if I release this attachment?* Often, loosening one grip reveals options that were invisible while you were clenched. Name what you see now.

If staying the course: Ask: *What needs to be renewed or strengthened for me to continue with integrity?* Staying the course isn't the same as grinding forward unchanged. What support, resources, or recommitment does this path require?

Identify one concrete action you can take within the next day. Small enough to complete, specific enough to know when you've done it.

Pay attention to the results; they are your confirmation. If they aren't aligned with your expectations, reassess.

Adaptations

Quick version (3 minutes): When you notice grip, pause. Three sigh breaths with the sip at the top. Ask only: "What am I attached to?" and "Release or stay the course?" Let your body answer.

Deep version (20+ minutes): Journal through each phase. Spend extended time mapping your tension patterns. Write a dialogue with the part of your body holding the most grip. Explore the history of this particular attachment. Where does it keep appearing in your life?

Walking version: Take the practice outside. Walk slowly. Let each phase correspond to a segment of your walk. Physical movement often releases what sitting cannot.

Partner version: Have someone you trust guide you through the questions. Ask them to notice your body language and reflect what they see.

What to Expect

First few times: Your mind will resist the emptiness. You'll feel the urge to check your phone, make a mental list, or solve something. Restlessness is normal. Your nervous system has been trained for constant stimulation. Each time you return to the breath or the open awareness, you're building greater capacity. Some sessions will feel like nothing happened. The work is happening beneath the surface.

After practicing it a few times: Entry into stillness becomes faster. Your body learns the cues. You'll start to recognize the felt sense of each phase and move through them more fluidly. Insights begin arriving not just during practice but throughout your day, as if the stillness you've cultivated keeps working in the background.

Pay attention to the results around you. Results will show the impact of your actions. If they aren't aligned with your expectations, reassess.

Common Obstacles

"I can see the attachment, but I can't release it." Seeing is the first step, not the final one. Ask: "What is this attachment protecting?" Often, we grip because something feels unsafe. Address the underlying safety concern, and the grip may soften on its own.

"I genuinely don't know whether to let go or stay." When unclear, the answer is usually "not yet." Return to the practice tomorrow. Ask: "Who do I trust, that can see what I'm missing?" Clarity often arrives when we stop demanding an immediate answer, or when we get help from someone we trust.

Field Note

Angela's four-year relationship had ended three months earlier. The separation was still raw; the wounds still close to the surface.

One evening, scrolling through social media, she saw her ex-partner had posted a video. The message was general, something about integrity and knowing who you can trust. But the moment Angela saw it, her chest tightened. She was certain it was about her. She spent the next hour composing responses in her head, defending herself against accusations he hadn't actually made.

When we talked the next day, she was still activated. I asked her to slow down. Was there any evidence the post was directed at her? She admitted there wasn't. He had a large following. The message could have been a general statement about how we treat each other as people. She had assumed herself into the center of it.

I walked her through the letting go practice. First, we worked with her body, slowing her breathing until the grip in her chest began to soften. Then the skillful inquiry: What are you attached to here? What are you trying to control that isn't in your control?

She realized she was holding tight to how he perceived her, something she could never manage from the outside.

As her body relaxed and her mind quieted, a deeper question became available. If the post wasn't about her, why had she reacted so strongly? The trigger had exposed something in her.

We looked at her values and whether her actions during the separation had aligned with them. What emerged surprised her. She had been carrying guilt about being the one who initiated the breakup. Had she been too cold? Avoidant when she could have been present? The post hadn't accused her of anything. It had simply landed on a bruise she hadn't known was there.

But when we examined what had actually happened, she discovered she hadn't been outside her values during the process. She had ended the relationship with as much care as she could. The guilt she was carrying didn't match the reality of how she had behaved. She wouldn't have uncovered this without seeing that post. The trigger was the flashlight that illuminated her work.

Remember This

Letting go isn't defeat. It's opening to possibilities that exist beyond your current vision.

Your body knows first. When effort stops producing results, when exhaustion doesn't improve with rest, when you've lost connection to your original purpose, these are signals worth heeding.

Feng Sung, connected relaxation, is the art of releasing your grip while maintaining your direction. You're not collapsing. You're not giving up. You're softening enough to let new information in and adjust your route without abandoning your destination.

The practice is developing wisdom to know when holding on serves you and when letting go would serve you better.

4

SLOW IS THE FAST WAY

Who can remain still, until clarity emerges?
Who can remain at peace, until the moment to act reveals itself?
— Lao Tzu

A heron stands motionless at the edge of a quiet lake. Its stillness emerges from diamond-clear purpose. Its eyes fixed on the water beneath. Ripples distort the underwater world while fish dart in seemingly random patterns. Yet from its stillness, the heron sees through the chaos. It recognizes the rhythm of the water and the movement of life, choosing its moment with precision.

This stillness is not passive. It pulses with awareness, intent, and focus. The heron demonstrates what we will explore throughout this chapter: that our greatest effectiveness comes not from constant action but from cultivating deliberate states of stillness that allow us to see more deeply, think more clearly, and act more effectively. This same stillness that brings clarity also opens doorways to creative insights we could never force through effort alone.

You've experienced this. You wrestle with a problem all day, getting nowhere. You give up, step into the shower, and halfway through shampooing your hair, the answer arrives. Unbidden. Complete. As if it had been waiting for you to stop trying.

Or you lie awake at 2 AM, cycling through the same problem, the same dead ends. Eventually exhaustion wins and you fall asleep. By morning, something has shifted. The path forward is clear.

We treat these moments as accidents. Fortunate coincidences. But they're not random. They're evidence of a different kind of intelligence that only activates when we stop forcing.

During the pandemic, when I closed my medical practice and Qigong studio, my family and I relocated to a small house in Upstate New York. The house sat at the base of a beautiful grassy hill at the edge of the woods. On the plateau at its summit, we created what became our outdoor living room, complete with comfortable lawn furniture, a fire pit, and a natural canopy of oak and maple trees circling it.

In the afternoons, I would climb up to this sanctuary, often lying on one of the couches, watching the clouds drift through the circular opening in the tree canopy above. The breeze would rustle through the leaves, creating a symphony that shifted with the changing seasons. It was like looking through a living lens to the sky, the trees forming a perfect frame for the ever-changing tableau of clouds above.

At first, these afternoon retreats felt like guilty pleasure. "Shouldn't I be doing something more productive?" I would think. That question carried a familiar weight in my chest, a tightness I recognized from decades of building practices, seeing patients, teaching classes. There was always something that needed to be done. Lying on a couch watching clouds felt like betrayal of everything I had been taught about earning my place in the world.

But I kept returning. And after a while, I began to notice a pattern. I would find myself drawn to this spot when wrestling with complex problems or decisions that seemed to have no clear solution. Instead of actively trying to solve these challenges, I would let them sit in the back of my mind while I watched the clouds drift by. I would feel myself step into the creative drift, and then without expectation, an answer would surface.

One afternoon, sitting up on that hill watching the changing sky and thinking about what the next phase of my career would be, I realized that after twenty-five years of practicing medicine, I was done. I never would have been able to make a logical argument for that choice. But when it came to me, I knew it was true. When you have one of these moments and you feel that sense of resonance, hold it close. It's easy for these realizations to slip away, but they are the voice of your deepest and clearest self.

Stillness in a World of Constant Motion

Peter Bregman, the executive coach and author of *Four Seconds*, puts it this way: "Being bored is a precious thing, a state of mind we should pursue. Once boredom sets in, our minds begin to wander, looking for something exciting, something interesting to land on. And that's where creativity is born."

What Bregman describes as boredom, neuroscience reveals as the activation of our default mode network. This is the brain state where creative connections happen that focused effort cannot produce. The same neural circuitry that feels like "doing nothing" is actually performing sophisticated work beneath conscious awareness, connecting distant ideas, rehearsing possibilities, and weaving fragments of memory into new insight.

Stillness sounds simple, even obvious. But when was the last time you allowed yourself to be truly still, without an objective? How long could you resist checking your phone, initiating conversation, moving around, or creating some form of action? In our society, we equate action with value and impact, especially when it produces visible results. Inaction becomes synonymous with laziness, lack of ambition, or apathy. If we stay locked in this limited equation, we keep ourselves from discovering the hidden value of intentional stillness.

When companies face complex challenges, leaders typically call for more activity: additional meetings, increased communication, expanded deliverables. Yet research consistently demonstrates that innovative solutions emerge most readily when teams create deliberate pauses in their workflow. These are not vacations or breaks, but structured moments of observation and integration.

The current workplace has effectively eliminated the natural pauses that once punctuated our days, creating gaps in activity. Whether waiting in line, sitting on public transportation, taking a walk, or transitioning between activities, now all those spaces are filled with scrolling, tapping, and streaming that keep our task-focused brain networks continuously engaged. The average person checks their phone ninety-six times per day. Each of these micro-interruptions fragments attention and prevents our minds from entering the reflective, associative states of stillness that are required for creative connection.

This is really hard in a world where digital platforms are deliberately engineered to hijack our attention. Through their gamified reward mechanisms, they use the same psychological loops that underlie most forms of addiction. We receive dopamine hits from likes, notifications, and novelty. The result is a powerful incentive system that makes stillness feel unsatisfying.

As you practice stillness, your skill will develop quickly. Your body will learn to move into states of deep relaxation and nourishment. From this open, settled place, your priorities shift. You stop hunting for the next reward and start thinking in longer horizons, toward creative strategies that yield greater impact and more lasting value.

In my experience with clients, chasing dopamine has become one of the most common obstacles to stillness. Seeking satisfaction, getting bored, reaching for the next thing. Buddhists call this craving. It's a terminal state of wanting that makes it impossible to enjoy just being alive.

The technology researcher Linda Stone famously described this modern condition as "continuous partial attention": a state where we're never fully engaged with a single task but also never fully disengaged enough to allow our deeper creative networks to activate. This isn't just a matter of willpower or discipline. The digital environment we've created is fundamentally at odds with the neurological conditions required for both deep self-awareness and creative insight.

The Three Levels of Stillness

Research reveals that stillness operates on a continuum, with different lengths of time offering distinct benefits. Understanding stillness as a multilevel capacity transforms how we approach it. Rather than seeing stillness as a single state to achieve, we can develop progressive skills that build upon each other, each serving different purposes in our development.

Level One: Regulatory Stillness (1—5 minutes)

At this foundational level, we activate the parasympathetic nervous system, the rest and digest response that counteracts the stress dominating much of our daily lives. This is more than just a feeling of calm. Measurable physiological changes occur: blood pressure decreases, cortisol levels drop, and the immune system functions more efficiently.

The journey into stillness begins with these brief periods where you slow your breath, let the tension drain from your body, and allow your mind to come fully into the present experience. When I work with clients, I begin every session with this centering reset. It allows both of us to arrive in the present moment together and release whatever was happening previously.

Life constantly demands context switching, often without adjustment periods. The micro-stillness practice provides a beautiful and effective ritual to end one state of mind and experience what comes next with greater presence and mental clarity.

Level Two: Contemplative Stillness (5—20 minutes)

As we sustain stillness, deeper changes emerge. Research from the University of Wisconsin-Madison's Center for Healthy Minds demonstrates that even short periods of mindfulness practice create measurable changes in behavior. These shifts are reflected in patterns of brain activity, especially in regions supporting attention, emotional regulation, and executive decision-making. Regular contemplative practice correlates with increased cortical thickness in the prefrontal cortex, essential for complex reasoning and self-governance.

Once you have developed a skillful practice with micro-stillness and can quiet the surface layer of your thoughts with ease, a state of much deeper stillness becomes available to you. This practice allows you to quiet your prefrontal cortex, turning off your reasoning and problem-solving mind while opening intuition. This is the skill that activates the intuitive capacity we explored in Chapter 1 through Shen listening.

The progression follows a natural development on the path of stillness. You began with micro-practices that down-regulate your nervous system. As these become habitual, your capacity for stillness grows. What starts as a micro-intervention grows into a powerful skill, building the ability to remain steady, spacious, and creative.

When we access deeper stillness, we see past reactivity into what's actually present. Leaders who cultivate this capacity lead from genuine presence rather than habitual patterns. But the deepest gift isn't strategic. It's relational. Stillness allows us to truly see and connect with the people around us. For leaders, this is how we keep people engaged, how we understand what they need to grow, and how we become of service to them. When people feel genuinely seen, their hearts and minds open. They become more engaged, more committed, and more willing to grow.

Level Three: Creative Stillness (20+ minutes)

Extended periods of stillness activate what neuroscientist Dr. Srini Pillay calls the "magnificent" default mode network. Far from being idle, this hidden circuitry becomes the stage where the mind rehearses its most intricate performances, connecting distant ideas, sketching possibilities not yet lived, and stitching fragments of memory into a larger tapestry of meaning. It supports mental time travel, self-reflection, and the gentle weaving of insight from what once felt like scattered threads. It is like a brilliant assistant who organizes everything behind the scenes that can only step forward when you finally turn away.

Dr. Kelly McGonigal's aggregated research adds another dimension to our understanding. She noticed that what happens in our brains during these "unproductive" moments is actually essential for innovation and problem-solving. The brain's default mode network, which scientists used to dismiss as just an "idle" state, is actually working overtime during these periods, creating connections that simply can't emerge when we're pushing hard with focused effort.

Think of those moments when you surrendered to doing nothing, watching clouds drift, meandering without purpose, or letting your gaze blur in a crowd, when suddenly, without effort, the answer to a question that you had been stuck on earlier pops into your mind.

The pattern of creative emergence follows a predictable arc. At first, there's resistance: the mind chatters, the body fidgets, and we feel an almost irresistible urge to "do something." This is followed by a period of settling, where the initial resistance begins to fade and we start to notice details in our environment we previously missed. Finally, we enter the creative drift, a state where the boundaries between problem and solution become fluid, and insights arrive through intuition and inspiration.

Cloud Watching: A Gateway Practice

Cloud watching became my gateway practice for the executives I coached. Without fail, the most analytically brilliant leaders would resist this simple instruction at first. Everyone wants fancy tools from their coaches, but the simplest are often the most effective. This was the lesson they needed most: learning to deliberately step away from the relentless drive of focused execution and allow their minds to drift into that fertile space where the default mode network awakens.

The practice itself was easy. Find a comfortable spot, look up at the clouds, and let your mind wander without an agenda for fifteen minutes. No checking phones, no mental list-making, just pure observation dissolving into reverie. What emerged from these sessions consistently surprised them. Problems that had seemed intractable would suddenly reveal elegant solutions. Connections between disparate ideas would crystallize. Most importantly, they would access Shen listening, that intuitive knowing that transcends analytical thought.

This becomes especially crucial when navigating complexity. Whether facing a strategic inflection point or a life-changing decision, we discover that our habitual mode of attacking problems with more analysis often creates more confusion. But when we cultivate deliberate moments of drift, whether through cloud watching, aimless walks, or simply sitting without purpose, we create the neurological conditions for breakthrough thinking. Our consciousness can finally access those deeper patterns and possibilities that remain invisible when we're locked in task-oriented thinking.

Think of it like this: if you're stuck on a problem, make three columns: one for pros, one for cons, and one for intuition. After you've listed the pros and cons, do this practice and see what arises in the third column.

Will, a CEO of a New York hedge fund I worked with, exemplified the transformation this practice can create. He had built the epitome of a successful financial career: brilliant analyst, driven leader, founder of his own fund. When we met, he knew he was ready for a big shift. He wanted to leave the fund he had started and step into the next phase of his life. If you've ever found yourself in this moment, you know it's terrifying. Not just to step away from something you're successful at, but to recognize that something greater is calling you forward, and into the unknown.

The skills that move you into this next stage often run counter to the skills that got you there. For Will, high execution, relentless work, ruthlessness when necessary: these qualities and the drive that accompanied them were his recipe for success. Now they would become his biggest obstacles.

When I first suggested he spend twenty minutes a day lying on his deck watching clouds, you can probably imagine his response.

"I want strategies for what I should do and how I should do it. I need tools that are actually going to get me where I need to go."

"But you don't know where you want to go," I said. "You only know it's different than where you are. So first we have to spend time being here. Opening up. Letting the future reveal itself in the present. And to do that, we have to let your mind get bored. Stop letting it run its normal loops."

It was counterintuitive, but he decided to trust me.

He began incorporating these periods of intentional boredom into his routine. Then he started to notice a shift. He began to realize that he didn't have to stop being who he was to grow into his next phase. His skills would always be with him, but he needed to let them move to the background while he aligned with his next vision. Will went on to create an influential fund that has shifted how the world sees psilocybin and other plant medicines as a means of healing, growth, and higher consciousness.

A Medical Breakthrough Born from Pause

What becomes possible when we stop forcing solutions?

At Memorial Sloan Kettering Cancer Center, oncologists Dr. Andrea Cercek and Dr. Luis Diaz faced a familiar challenge. Rectal cancer patients with a specific tumor type were being treated with the standard aggressive trio: chemotherapy, radiation, and surgery. The protocols worked to varying degrees, but at a serious cost to the patient's quality of life. Things like bowel and bladder dysfunction, infertility, and chronic pain, to name a few.

The conventional path forward would have been incremental. Refine the dosing. Improve surgical techniques. Reduce side effects at the margins. Instead, the team paused long enough to ask a different kind of question: What if the immune system alone, given the right support, could resolve the cancer without any of this?

It was the kind of question that doesn't survive a busy schedule. It requires stillness. Space. The willingness to sit with not-knowing long enough for something unexpected to surface.

They proposed an unconventional trial: treating patients exclusively with an immunotherapy drug. No chemo. No radiation. No surgery.

Every patient in that early trial experienced remission. This created a paradigm shift in the treatment of rectal cancer and inspired a whole new wave of cancer innovation.

This is what creative stillness makes possible. Not incrementally better answers to the same questions, but entirely new questions that dissolve the problem as originally framed.

Practice: The Stillness Cascade

Applied Insights

The capacity to move from surface noise into progressively deeper states of stillness where clarity, intuition, and creative insight become accessible. This practice trains your nervous system to quiet on command and opens the default mode network where breakthrough thinking occurs. Over time, you develop the ability to access stillness quickly, even under pressure.

When to Use

- When your mind is spinning but nothing resolves
- When you need creative insight that analytical thinking can't produce
- Before making significant decisions
- When you feel depleted and need restoration beyond rest
- When a problem has resisted every approach you've tried
- As a daily centering practice

The Practice

Find 15-30 minutes in a quiet space where you won't be interrupted. You can do this seated or lying down. Before beginning, acknowledge what you're bringing to this practice. You might have a specific challenge you're hoping for insight on, or you might simply need restoration. Either is fine. If you have a question or problem, hold it lightly in the back of your mind without actively working on it. The practice will do its work whether you arrive with an agenda or without one.

Phase One: Settling the Body

Sit or lie in a comfortable position with your spine supported. Begin extending your exhale longer than your inhale. Breathe in for a count of four, out for a count of six (Keep the counting pace the same). Continue for a few minutes, gradually extending the exhale further until you reach a long but comfortable exhale and feel yourself starting to relax. This activates your vagus nerve and shifts your nervous system from activation to receptivity. From doing, to being.

Feel the rhythm of your breath in the rise and fall of your belly. Let your attention rest there rather than chasing thoughts. When your mind pulls toward planning or problem-solving, return to the sensation of your breath. Stay here until you feel your body genuinely settle. Not performing relaxation, but actually arriving in it.

Phase Two: Softening the Mind

Once your body has settled, let your hands rest wherever it is comfortable. Allow your attention to expand from the breath into open awareness. You're not focusing on any particular object. You're creating spacious noticing.

If you brought a challenge or question to this practice, let it exist in this space without working on it. Hold it the way you hold an egg: Tight enough that you don't drop it, but loose enough that it doesn't break. If thoughts arise about the challenge, notice them and let them pass like clouds. You're not blocking your thoughts. You're not following them either.

This is where soft fascination begins. Your mind might drift to memories, images, or seemingly unrelated ideas. These aren't distractions. They're your deeper intelligence beginning to activate. Notice without grasping.

Phase Three: The Creative Drift

Now release even the light holding from Phase Two. Let your attention go wherever it wants. Step into your cloud watching mind. Purposeless. Receptive. Allowing.

Your default mode network activates when you stop effortful thinking. This is where your brain makes connections your conscious mind cannot force. Solutions arrive not as logical conclusions but as creative or sudden inspiration; unexpected metaphors, or perspective shifts in how you see the entire situation.

You might think about childhood. You might see patterns in the ceiling. You might feel emotions arise without a clear cause. Stay with whatever comes. This apparent randomness is your brain conducting a sophisticated search through vast networks of association. **Trust the drift**.

Phase Four: Gathering

When you sense the practice completing, whether through time or natural resolution, don't jump immediately back into activity. Stay in the transition.

Notice what came up. Just note what surfaced. Images, memories, feelings, phrases, ideas. If something feels significant, write it down before it fades.

Then ask: *How has my relationship to the question or challenge shifted?* Often the insight isn't a direct answer but a reframing that makes the original problem dissolve or reveal itself as the wrong question.

Take nine slow, deep breaths, this time making the inhale longer than the exhale. Let the stillness integrate before re-entering motion.

Adaptations

Quick version: When you need a reset between activities. Both hands on your belly, extend the exhale for a minute or two until your body settles. Then two minutes of open awareness without an agenda. One minute to notice what's different before moving on.

Deep version: Extended creative drift. Set a timer so you don't monitor the time. Let yourself fall into the space between waking and sleeping where insight often lives. Journal immediately upon completion.

Walking version: Slow walking in a quiet space. Phase One while standing still. Then walk at half your normal pace, letting your soft gaze and open awareness move with you. Some people access creative drifts more easily in gentle motion.

Passenger version: Riding in a car, train, or bus as a passenger. Let your gaze soften out the window, watching the landscape pass without tracking or analyzing it. The movement and changing scenery naturally quiet the analytical mind and invite the drift state.

Before-sleep version: Practice Phases One and Two in bed. Let Phase Three carry you into sleep. Keep a notebook nearby. Insights often surface upon waking.

What to Expect

First few times: Your mind will resist the emptiness. You'll feel the urge to check your phone, make a mental list, or solve something. Restlessness is normal. Your nervous system has been trained for constant stimulation. Each time you return to the breath or the open awareness, you're building new capacity. Some sessions will feel like nothing happened. The work is happening beneath the surface.

After a few times of doing the practice: Entry into stillness becomes faster. Your body learns the cues. You'll start to recognize the felt sense of each phase and move through them more fluidly. Insights begin arriving not just during practice but throughout your day, as if the stillness you've cultivated keeps working in the background.

Pay attention to what the stillness opens for you. The impact is in the results. If they aren't aligned with your expectations, reassess.

Common Obstacles

"My mind won't stop." It doesn't need to stop. The goal isn't a blank mind but a mind that isn't chasing or grasping. Thoughts will arise. Let them pass without following. Each time you notice you've been hooked by a thought and return to open awareness, that's the practice working.

"I fall asleep." This often means you're genuinely exhausted, and your body is taking what it needs. Let yourself sleep. Over time, as you become more rested, you'll find the edge between deep relaxation and sleep where creative stillness lives. If you keep falling asleep, try sitting upright rather than lying down.

Field Note

When I'm working with people who are new to stillness practices, I've found that one simple adjustment makes the transition much easier.

The constant stimulation we're used to creates almost a mini withdrawal that we have to move through in order to get the value of the practice.

One easy way to get around this is to put light music on that has no words. Something that can bring you into a particular mood or state. The music gives your mind just enough to pay attention to, something of no real consequence, but it allows your mind and body to guide themselves into the quieting down stage faster.

So, think of this: if you're having trouble just being in the stillness at the beginning of the cascade, let yourself start to go into that space by putting on some music.

Remember This

Stillness isn't passive. It's where your deepest intelligence activates.

Three levels serve different purposes: regulatory stillness (1—5 minutes) resets your nervous system, contemplative stillness (5—20 minutes) opens intuition, and creative stillness (20+ minutes) unlocks breakthrough insight.

The default mode network that feels like "doing nothing" is actually performing sophisticated work beneath conscious awareness. Solutions that won't come through effort arrive when you stop forcing.

In a world that never stops moving, your edge might be your capacity to be still.

5

ADAPTIVE RESPONSE

"Can you hold body and spirit together without losing their unity?"
— Lao Tzu

In the previous chapter, we looked at how the mind predicts and filters reality. Now we step back and examine the deeper architecture that built that system and the evolutionary wiring that shaped it. You carry ancient programming refined over millions of years. Your stress responses, your social instincts, and your pattern recognition were all shaped by environments that no longer exist. This programming isn't a flaw to fix. It's intelligence to work with.

This chapter is about that partnership. Adaptive Intelligence is your capacity to consciously work with your wiring by bringing it into the foreground of your awareness. It's the ability to read your stress responses as intelligent signals, to understand the cycles your body moves through in stressful situations and respond in ways that align with who you want to be, rather than being driven by an unconscious biological response.

This is different from resilience as most people understand it. Resilience often gets framed as toughening up, pushing through, bouncing back.

Adaptive Intelligence is something else. It's recognizing that you are a living system, not a machine. You are meant to move through cycles, not hold one phase indefinitely.

A few years ago, I was driving to a retreat in Northern California and decided to stop at the Redwood Forest along the way. Standing among these 2000-year-old giants, I found myself thinking about the nature of adaptation and change. Here was a living example of something that had survived and thrived through countless environmental shifts, wars, technological revolutions, and climate variations. The forest had witnessed the rise and fall of civilizations, yet it remained, constantly adapting while maintaining its essential nature.

Some trees were ancient giants, some were middle-aged and thriving, some were saplings just beginning their journey. Some of them had died and fallen down, returning their nutrients to the soil. This forest was a flexible system in constant change, creating balance across millennia.

Cycles Within Cycles

Ecologists developed the concept of Panarchy to describe how complex adaptive systems move through recurring cycles of growth, conservation, release, and reorganization. The Redwood Forest demonstrates this perfectly. New growth pushes upward, capturing resources, and expanding. Mature trees consolidate, becoming stable and efficient. Eventually, old growth falls, releasing nutrients back into the system. And from that release, reorganization begins, making space for new life.

Think of how firefighters use controlled burns to prevent catastrophic wildfires. They don't wait for dead wood and undergrowth to accumulate until a lightning strike creates an inferno. Instead, they deliberately create small, manageable strategic fires during safe conditions to remove the fuel for future forest fires. They work with the cycle rather than against it.

These same cycles operate in our bodies, our careers, our relationships. We go through periods of rapid growth and expansion. We consolidate and stabilize. We release what's no longer serving us. We reorganize and begin again. The challenge is that most of us fight these natural rhythms rather than working with them. We try to stay in perpetual growth. We resist release. We fear reorganization.

The leaders I work with who navigate change most skillfully understand these cycles intuitively. They plant new initiatives while others are maturing. They sunset products gracefully while new ones are emerging. They evolve, and because of that evolution, they thrive. Those who don't evolve, who try to freeze the cycle in one phase, ultimately fail.

Ancient Software, Modern World

The deeper challenge we face is that we're trying to navigate unprecedented rates of change using an operating system that evolved for a very different world. Our brains and bodies were shaped by millions of years of evolution in environments where change happened gradually, where the skills your great-grandparents developed remained relevant for their children and grandchildren. Now we face a world where entire industries can transform in a few years, where the half-life of specific skills is shrinking every year, where we must constantly reinvent ourselves while somehow maintaining a coherent sense of who we are.

Our minds are prediction machines, constantly creating shortcuts and patterns from limited data. This was an evolutionary advantage when the patterns were stable. It becomes a liability when those predictions go unchecked or when our environment changes faster than our perceptual frameworks can adapt.

The hypervigilance I developed around my father is a case in point. Decades later, that childhood programming was still running. We can rewrite these patterns, but first we have to see how deep they go.

We all carry early patterning like this. Sometimes dramatic, sometimes subtle. Unless we work with it consciously, our nervous system keeps responding as if the old world is still the current one. The patterns that protected you in one phase of life may distort your perception in another. Conscious recalibration is periodically necessary and always possible.

The Snowstorm

I discovered the full power of this ancient programming on a mountain road in Colorado, where technology and nature conspired to create a perfect laboratory for understanding how our evolutionary inheritance still shapes our response to life's challenges.

I was sitting in the Walmart parking lot in Frisco, Colorado, surrounded by shopping bags filled with supplies I hoped I wouldn't need. Extra wool socks, thermal gloves, chemical hand warmers, emergency blankets, water bottles, energy bars, and a flashlight. My brand-new electric car hummed quietly as it charged, its dashboard displaying a cheerful green battery icon that seemed absurdly optimistic given what I was about to attempt.

Twenty minutes earlier, I had been confidently following my car's navigation app on what was supposed to be a straightforward drive to Crestone. The algorithm had plotted what I thought was an efficient route based on charging station locations, sending me through the Eisenhower Tunnel to this charging stop in Frisco. Only when I checked the next leg of the journey did I realize what that app had planned for me: a narrow mountain pass road that wound through a section of Colorado's remote mountain terrain. The same algorithm that could calculate my battery consumption to the decimal point had somehow failed to factor in the narrow curvy roads and the blizzard outside.

Standing in that Walmart, grabbing supplies off the shelves, I became a case study of the autonomic nervous system in action. I could feel my nervous system switching into overdrive. My heart rate spiking, breath shallow, mouth dry, and my emotional brain hyper-focused on survival gear.

The freeze response came first, that moment in the parking lot when I initially realized what lay ahead. For several seconds, I simply stood still, unable to decide whether to go on or turn back. This freezing response served our ancestors well. When you detect a potential threat but aren't sure of how dangerous it is or where it is, freezing prevents you from attracting attention while your brain rapidly assesses the situation. In my case, this looked like standing motionless in the parking lot, keys in hand, staring at my phone's weather radar.

After the freeze came the fight response. Not against another person but against the situation itself. I found myself angry at the conditions, gripping the shopping cart tightly, moving through the store with aggressive efficiency. "I'll show this storm," I muttered, loading up on supplies as if preparing for battle. My muscles were tense, jaw clenched, ready for confrontation with an enemy that was really just frozen water falling from the sky.

Throughout this preparation, the third response lurked in the background: flight. Every few minutes, the thought would surface: "Just turn around. Find a hotel. Wait it out." This urge to escape, to avoid the challenge entirely, pulled at me with surprising strength. Even as I loaded supplies into my car, part of my brain was calculating alternate routes, considering excuses I could make for arriving a day late, imagining the warm safety of simply not attempting this journey.

During that three-hour drive through the blizzard, I experienced every aspect of this ancient response. When visibility dropped to mere feet and I could no longer see the edge of the road, the freeze response would grip me. I would slow to a crawl, hands white-knuckled around the steering wheel, unable to decide whether stopping or continuing posed greater risk. The fight response emerged as I wrestled with the car's handling on ice, leaning forward aggressively, gripping the wheel as if I could force the vehicle to obey through sheer will. The flight impulse remained constant, a background voice suggesting I pull over at the next town, find somewhere safe to wait.

I made it to Crestone, exhausted and exhilarated. I felt triumphant as the last of the adrenaline carried me into the house.

The System Underneath

The irony of that day wasn't lost on me. There I was, navigating one of nature's genuine challenges in a vehicle that represented the pinnacle of modern technology, guided by satellites orbiting the Earth, yet my body was responding exactly as it would have if I were a settler in the 1800s crossing the Oregon Trail. My sympathetic nervous system didn't care that I had heated seats and GPS tracking.

This is the paradox. The same responses that once kept us alive can now hijack our effectiveness.

The freeze that would hide you from a tiger in the wild can make you miss opportunities in your life. The fight that would mobilize you for combat can also make you send an email you will later regret. The flight that removes you from danger can make you avoid the very conversation you need to have.

Research shows that when these stress responses activate repeatedly without recovery, the costs accumulate. The body carries higher levels of inflammation. The mind loses flexibility. The brain regions we depend on for clarity and judgment begin to falter. What researchers call "allostatic load," the cumulative wear on the mind and body from repeated stress cycles, has become endemic in modern life.

The goal isn't to shut these responses off. You can't. The goal is to recognize them as intelligent systems and learn to work with them.

The Stress Paradox

It turns out that we have been missing a crucial piece of information around stress. It doesn't have to be bad for us.

This insight came to me through a few different studies that Kelly McGonigal connected in a lecture, whose research on stillness we explored in the previous chapter. McGonigal also highlighted research showing that our beliefs about stress are critical to its impact on our health.

In a large U.S. study tracking nearly 30,000 adults over eight years, researchers asked participants two simple questions: How much stress had they experienced in the past year, and did they believe stress was harmful to their health? They then matched those responses with public death records.

The results were striking. People who reported high stress and believed stress was harmful had a 43 percent higher risk of death. But those who experienced high stress without viewing it as harmful showed no increased risk of mortality. Believing stress is harmful was associated with higher mortality risk, especially among highly stressed individuals.

This finding offers a powerful new viewpoint on how we can manage our stress. It turns out our framing of stress as harmful or not can powerfully influence its impact on our bodies.

In a study from 2010 at Harvard called *Rethink Your Stress*, participants were taught to rethink their stress response as helpful. When stressed, your heart is pounding, preparing you for action. Your breathing speeds up to bring more oxygen to your brain. Before going through a stressful test, the participants were told these physical responses were their bodies' way of energizing them and preparing them to perform well.

As you might imagine, the results were positive. Not only did participants feel less anxious and more confident, but their physical response to stress changed. Yes, their hearts were still pounding, but blood vessels stayed relaxed. Instead of the cardiovascular profile of fear, they showed the profile of courage. This meant things like, although their heart was beating much faster, their blood vessels remained dilated, and blood flow circulated more effectively through their bodies. Whereas in the negative framing of stress, our blood vessels would constrict, blood pressure would go up, and circulation would go down. The takeaway is this: When you reframe stress in this way, you get the benefits of the physiological changes, but you remove a lot of the negatives.

Same physiology. Different belief. Different outcome.

There's one last piece of the stress equation that shows us the eloquent design of our bodies. It's oxytocin. Most people know it as the cuddle hormone, but your body also releases it during stress. It primes you for connection: reaching out for help, seeking support, and caring for others.

Oxytocin doesn't just act on your brain. It has receptors in your cardiovascular system, where it can help regenerate cells and heal from stress-induced damage. Your body's stress response has a built-in mechanism for resilience and healing. That mechanism is human connection.

So next time you're stressed, open up, get vulnerable, reach out to someone to talk to, or get a hug.

McGonigal points to another study that tracked about 1,000 adults in the United States. Researchers asked how much stress participants had experienced in the last year and how much time they spent helping out friends, neighbors, or people in their community. Then they used public records to find out who died over the next five years.

For every major stressful life experience, like financial difficulty or family crisis, the risk of dying increased by 30 percent. But people who spent time caring for others showed no stress-related increase in dying. Caring creates resilience.

When I bring this work to my clients, we stop talking only about reducing stress, and we start asking: What does this stress feel like? How am I thinking about it? Am I sharing the weight of leadership with my team?

The best way to use this tool is to build rituals that emphasize connection. Short check-ins, ceremonies to start and complete intense projects, and share the problem you're trying to solve with those who you trust. Athletes and performers swear by this technique and use it all the time when they're getting psyched up and ready to perform or compete in an event. They'll reframe everything that they're experiencing physiologically as the excitement that comes with the thrill of the challenge that they're facing. They visualize themselves, succeeding and performing at their highest level before they head out on stage or into the competition.

Where Your Programming Shows Up

This evolutionary inheritance doesn't affect us uniformly. In my work with leaders and teams, I've noticed it tends to concentrate in four areas.

Threat response is the most obvious. The executive who can't make decisions under pressure, or who makes them too fast without enough information. Their survival brain is either freezing or fighting when the situation calls for something more nuanced. Your physical signals are the early warning system here. Learning to read them gives you a head start on recognizing when ancient programming has taken over.

Social alignment is more subtle but very powerful. We evolved in tribes where exclusion meant death. That programming still runs. The leader who doesn't want to hear a dissenting opinion. The team member who shapes their ideas to match whoever spoke last. The executive who builds consensus when they should be making a call. Or a fear of saying something that will label you as a "nonbeliever." All of these examples are that tribal brain trying to keep us safe in a group. Awareness of these impulses helps us to navigate it clearly.

Resource management shows up as hoarding. Not just money, but information, credit, opportunity. The leader who grew up with scarcity often can't recognize abundance when it's right in front of them. They stockpile when they should distribute. They protect when they should invest. Scarcity narratives passed down through families continue shaping perception long after actual scarcity has ended.

Pattern-recognition helped our ancestors predict danger and find food. Now when it misfires, we see threats that aren't there and miss opportunities that don't fit our existing mental models. The leader who's certain they know what's happening often can't see what's actually emerging.

Most of us have one or two domains where we're particularly susceptible. Knowing where you're susceptible and recognizing when you're having a habitual response to a pattern gives you a head start on catching yourself and pivoting before the ancient programming takes over.

The Other Side of Stress

Now that we've looked at what happens when the stress response activates, you understand on a basic level the biochemical and neurochemical states that occur. The other side of the coin is relaxation, creativity, joy, connection, and all the emotions that emerge when the stress response subsides.

Take a moment to notice how you feel just by reading these words:

Relaxation

Creativity

Joy

Connection

Even reading them can cause a shift in your energetic state and awareness. When you have a nice lunch on a Sunday afternoon, or you're sitting with a loved one holding hands, when you hug an old friend or look into the eyes of your pet, you naturally go into the relaxation response.

All of us know this moment. Your breath softens and deepens, your mind opens, and you feel your muscles relaxing. There's often a sense of new possibilities that starts to grow in your awareness. We love this place. It's what everyone is striving for. Our culture tends to teach us that deep relaxation and creativity can only occur under specific conditions like a retreat, on the weekend, or when we are sitting somewhere quietly. But the truth is, we have the tools to drop into that state of consciousness whenever we want.

This ability to recognize our automatic responses and then consciously shift them is the cornerstone of adaptive intelligence. While our autonomic system evolved for a world of immediate physical threats, our conscious mind gives us the capacity to override these ancient patterns and respond in ways more appropriate to our modern challenges.

This is the Feng Sung, the connected relaxation we explored in Chapter 3. Here it offers us a key to working with stress: Enough tension for information to flow easily, but not so much that we get stuck. Peak performance requires this balance. The whole system is designed to function in quick feedback loops that work best when there's enough tension, but not too much.

Think of the Ready Position in any sport. One of the key indicators of the Ready Position is that every joint is unlocked, allowing all the muscles throughout the body to be in communication without first having to unlock a joint for information to flow.

Next time you're watching a sports event, whether it's tennis, football, cricket, or boxing, notice the athletes before the match begins. Everyone enters a position where all their joints are unlocked, slightly bent so that they can pivot and move without having to initiate that first step.

Beyond Perpetual Summer

Standing in that Redwood Forest, I thought about all the leaders I work with who try to maintain their organizations in a state of perpetual summer. They want constant growth, constant productivity, and constant success. But the forest offers a different wisdom.

The tree doesn't fight its nature. It grows in spring, flourishes in summer, releases in autumn, and consolidates in winter. Each phase serves the whole. Each phase makes the next possible.

The same invitation extends to you. Not to eliminate stress or transcend your evolutionary programming, but to develop a conscious skillful relationship with it. To recognize when ancient patterns are running the show. To use the reframe that transforms threat into challenge. To activate the connection that builds resilience. To know which season is your particular edge and to watch for it.

The forest offers a two-thousand-year-old lesson written in every tree: True resilience comes not from fighting against natural cycles but from learning to dance with them.

PRACTICE: Adaptive Response

Applied Insights

The capacity to work with your stress response rather than against it. This practice trains you to move stress chemicals through your body the way they were designed to move, then channel that energy into clear thinking and connection. Over time, you develop the ability to transform what feels like a threat into fuel for resilience and effective action.

When to Use

- When you feel a sudden charge of tension, heat, or emotional activation
- When someone says something unexpected and you feel anger or fear rise
- When anxiety is building and you need to perform
- When you notice fight, flight, or freeze responses arising
- After a stressful event to complete the stress cycle
- When pressure is mounting and you need to stay effective

The Practice

This practice is different from the contemplative ones. It responds to stress that's already present in your body. Before you begin, name the trigger. You already know what happened. Putting it into words gives you something concrete to return to later in the practice, after you've cleared your system.

Phase One: Move the Chemicals

When stress hits, your body floods with chemicals designed to optimize you for running or fighting. That's why you feel muscle tension, especially in your hips and lower back. Your system is primed for explosive movement. The fastest way through stress is to give your body what it's asking for.

Do three rounds of five squats. Go deep enough that your hips and thighs engage fully. If squats aren't available, climb three flights of stairs, do jumping jacks, or anything that strongly uses your legs, hips, and core. The large muscle groups are where stress chemicals concentrate. Move them.

Don't skip this. The physical discharge is what allows the next phases to work.

Phase Two: Aggressive Breathing

After the movement, your body is ready to reset. Sit down with your feet on the ground, hands relaxed at your sides.

Take a deep, full inhale through your mouth, filling your belly and chest completely. Then exhale fully through your mouth, letting the breath release with force. Not a gentle sigh. A strong, complete emptying.

Do three rounds of five breaths this way. Deep inhale, forceful exhale through the mouth. You may feel lightheaded. That's normal. You're flushing your system. *Do five rounds if you're not feeling a shift.*

After the third round, let your breathing return to normal. Notice what's shifted in your body. The charge that felt overwhelming a few minutes ago should feel more manageable now.

Phase Three: Reframe

Now that the chemical flood has moved through, you're thinking brain is back online. This is where you shift your relationship with stress itself.

Place both hands on your belly. Feel your heart rate settling, your breath evening out.

Remember what the research shows: people who experience high stress but don't view it as harmful show no increased health risks. When you interpret your stress response as your body preparing you to meet a challenge, your physiology actually changes. Your blood vessels stay relaxed even as your heart beats faster. Instead of the cardiovascular profile of fear, you create the profile of courage. Same activation, different belief, different outcome in your body.

Recognize what just happened: your body activated to meet a challenge. The pounding heart was pumping oxygen to your brain. The heightened alertness was sharpening your focus. That wasn't a malfunction, that was your system doing exactly what it evolved to do.

Say to yourself: That activation meant I cared about what was happening. My body was preparing me to respond. Now I can use that preparation.

From this clearer state, ask: *What's actually needed here?* Not what your fear says. Not what your anger demands. What's actually needed.

Phase Four: Connect

Stress releases oxytocin alongside adrenaline. This primes you for connection. Instead of isolating after activation, use this built-in resilience mechanism.

Bring to mind someone who supports you. If possible, reach out. Send a brief message. Make a short call. Share that you just moved through something stressful. Even brief contact helps your system complete the stress cycle and builds resilience over time.

If reaching out isn't possible, think of a person who would be your ally in this moment, and imagine them there with you. If you have a question, imagine how they would advise you.

Phase Five: Act

Identify one concrete action to take from this resourced state.

The action might be having a conversation you were avoiding. Sending a message you've been drafting in your head. Taking the first step on something overwhelming. Or simply returning to your day with a cleared system. Name your action. Then do it.

Adaptations

Quick version (3 minutes): When stress hits, immediately do one round of twenty squats or climb two flights of stairs. Then one round of ten aggressive breaths. Ask: "What's actually needed here?" Act from there.

Desk version: When you can't leave your workspace, do wall sits or press your palms hard against your thighs for thirty seconds, three times. Then the breathing rounds. Not as effective as full movement, but better than staying frozen.

Pre-event version: Before a high-stakes situation, do the movement and breathing phases to preemptively clear your system. Arrive resourced rather than braced.

What to Expect

First few times: Moving when you feel stressed can seem counterintuitive, especially when you're at work or in public. You'll want to contract into the feeling, analyze it, or push it down. The aggressive breathing may feel strange or uncomfortable. Do it anyway. Notice how different you feel after the physical discharge compared to when you try to think your way through stress.

After a few times of doing the practice: You'll start recognizing activation earlier and reaching for movement before the stress peaks. The breathing becomes a reliable reset you use throughout your day. You'll notice stress completing rather than accumulating. Your recovery time shortens.

Common Obstacles

"I can't do squats in this situation." Find what you can do. Walk briskly to the bathroom and back. Climb whatever stairs are available. Do wall sits in a private space. Clench every muscle group from feet to face, hold for three breaths, then release. Do it three times.

"The physical part helped but I still feel activated." Do another round of movement and breathing. Some stress loads need more discharge than others. There's no limit on rounds. Keep going until your system settles enough to think clearly.

Field Note

Anne had just come out of a tough performance review. She'd been told she wasn't meeting expectations and given three months to show complete change. She walked into my office, angry and afraid.

"They blindsided me," she said. "Three months to transform or I'm out."

This is one of the harder moments to navigate. Our tendency, especially when we don't expect the blow, is to react with projection, fear, and anger.

We couldn't do squats in my office, so we sat down and did three rounds of twenty fast deep breaths. Within minutes, her nervous system settled into a calmer, more present state. Then we began the reframe.

"Your body is responding to the importance of keeping your job," I said. "But it's also flooded with questions: What's my value here? How could this happen to me? We need to go past that layer and ask two different questions: What was the value of this meeting? And what do you want for an outcome?"

Once we separated the feedback from her reactivity, Anne saw it clearly. There were genuine gaps she could choose to address or not. She also realized she didn't feel valued for what she was already providing. When we reached the second question, "What do you want?" Her answer came with clarity. She wanted to work in her zone of excellence: high-level customer service, people-facing relationships, and delivering value to clients.

From that clarity, she could choose her path without the cloud of fear or anger. She looked honestly at what was being asked and decided she wanted to find a company that valued her current strengths rather than grow into skills that didn't align with what she wanted.

The freedom came not from reactivity, not from "do whatever it takes to stay" or "screw these people, I'm leaving," but from answering with genuine clarity: What do I want? Anne moved on to a company that valued what she offered.

Remember This

You carry ancient programming refined over millions of years. This programming isn't a flaw to fix. It's intelligence to work with.

The stress response that once kept our ancestors alive can now hijack our effectiveness when it activates repeatedly without recovery. The freeze that hides you from a tiger makes you miss opportunities. The fight that mobilizes you for combat makes you send emails you regret. The flight that removes you from danger makes you avoid conversations you need to have.

Kelly McGonigal's research reveals the paradox at the heart of stress: our beliefs about it shape its effects on our bodies. People who experience high stress but don't view it as harmful show no increased health risks. The same physical activation that damages us when we interpret it as threat strengthens us when we interpret it as our body rising to meet a challenge.

Connection is our built-in healing mechanism. Oxytocin, released during stress, primes us for reaching out, strengthens relationships, and literally helps heart cells regenerate from stress-induced damage. Isolation during stress cuts us off from this resilience. Connection activates it.

6

DEFINE THE FIELD

"A person who does not know where he is does not know who he is."
— Wendell Berry

No matter who I am working with, from CEOs to someone stepping into a new chapter of their life, one thought consistently overwhelms them when we face transformation: "How will I get from where I am to where I'm going?" The journey often seems insurmountable when you think about the distance from where you are to where you want to go. It's like looking at a mountain that stands between you and your destination.

So how do we get through the unknown terrain? Two things. First, we begin. Our journey of a thousand miles begins by taking the first step onto our path. Second, we use a map.

What is a map? A map is a series of boundaries that, when aligned correctly, allow for the flow of movement and energy from one place to another. From one state of mind to another. From one state of life to another. To understand how to build a map, we must understand the nature of boundaries.

The Boundary Paradox

The most common mistake people make with boundaries is thinking that they will create conflict. It is as if a boundary is a fence you put up to keep someone out. But even fences have gates. Fences stop people from traversing onto someone else's land, but they also give them a clear understanding of where their own land is and where they belong.

When we "put up" a boundary, it often has an emotional charge associated with it. These moments usually arise when we are trying to stop something. If there is emotional tension, it's always because there is either a real or imagined power struggle. One person wants the boundary, and one doesn't. These situations are solved through communication and often arise when two different cultures clash.

But a boundary can just as easily help you keep something happening that you want. We all know that red means stop and green means go. These are boundaries we've agreed upon as a society when we're driving or crossing the street. They help us move through our towns with far fewer accidents and greater ease of movement.

The fundamental paradox of boundaries is that they both constrain and liberate. Like the banks of a river, they channel energy in specific directions, enabling greater momentum and flow than would be possible without their guidance. Understanding this dual nature is essential for creating boundaries that empower rather than simply restrict.

The Clarity of Constraint

What's curious about boundaries is how they can enhance our creative capacity rather than diminish it. Back in 1960, Bennett Cerf, the founder of Random House, made a bet with Theodore Geisel (Dr. Seuss) that he couldn't write an entertaining children's book using only 50 different words. Dr. Seuss took that bet, and the result was *Green Eggs and Ham*, which became not only his most successful book but one of the best-selling children's books of all time.

Think about that for a moment. The constraint of using only 50 words didn't limit Dr. Seuss's creativity. It channeled it, focused it, and made it more powerful. It's like our river metaphor: when water flows within defined banks, it moves with greater force and clarity than when it spreads thin across a floodplain. The boundaries don't diminish the water's power. They direct it toward its purpose.

This principle shows up everywhere once you start looking for it. Musicians working within the structure of a blues progression discover infinite variations. Haiku poets find unparalleled expression within seventeen syllables. Even in our bodies, we see this. Our joints work because they have limits to their range of motion. Without those constraints, we'd have no leverage, no ability to generate force, or create purposeful movement.

The neuroscience behind this is revealing something our ancestors understood intuitively. When we work within constraints, our brains engage differently. Our analytical, associative, and creative networks activate together. It's as if the boundaries form a creative pressure that transforms our thinking, much like how a narrow canyon transforms a gentle stream into rapids. Rather than overwhelming us with infinite possibilities, well-chosen boundaries give our creativity something to push against, creating the friction that sparks innovation.

Rivers and Mountains

This same principle of creative constraint plays out beautifully in nature. I often think about how rivers flow down mountains. It's one of the most elegant examples of boundaries creating something greater than either element alone could achieve. Water, by its nature, seeks the lowest point. It wants to flow downward. The mountain, by its nature, stands firm with its rocks, trees, and changing angles of descent.

Now watch what happens when these two forces meet. The mountain's boundaries don't stop the water. They guide it, channel it, give it purpose and direction. As the river winds around boulders and speeds through narrow passages, it carves out pools where fish can thrive and rapids where the water moves too fast for algae to grow, creating pure drinking water for wildlife. Over centuries, this dance between the flowing river and the steadfast mountain creates an entire ecosystem. The boundaries we create don't limit the experience of our lives. They expand its possibilities.

What strikes me about this relationship is how neither force compromises its essential nature. The water doesn't become less fluid, and the mountain doesn't become less solid. Instead, their interaction, their boundary meeting, creates something neither could achieve alone: fertile valleys, underground aquifers that feed crops, lakes that support entire communities. The constraint becomes the catalyst for abundance.

This natural wisdom translates directly into how we create culture in our organizations. Culture often boils down to something surprisingly simple: it is created every day by the behaviors that leaders demonstrate and reinforce. These behaviors become the boundaries, the riverbanks if you will, that guide how energy flows through the organization.

When everyone understands and shares these agreements, movement becomes almost effortless. You know when to stop, when to go, and when to yield. The boundaries don't restrict your journey. They make it possible to reach your destination without constant negotiation or conflict. Like the river flowing down the mountain, when our intentions are clear and we understand the terrain we're navigating, the path forward reveals itself naturally.

The Yellow Light Zone

You knew this part was coming. What happens when the light is yellow?

A yellow light is an unclear boundary. The color literally lives between red and green, and it creates a certain amount of confusion. I have a dear friend who is a glassblower, and he makes incredible chandeliers, fine Italian champagne flutes, and other-worldly sculptures that glow in the dark. They are quite beautiful. Sometimes, when we were looking at a piece that he made, and it had an imperfection in it, I'd ask him, "Are you OK with that imperfection there?" He would tell me that when he's making art and turning molten glass, there's a moment of uncertainty where something changes that wasn't planned. That often becomes the imperfection that is the signature uniqueness of the piece and wouldn't be discovered unless he decided to explore that moment of uncertainty.

What makes all of us beautiful is our imperfections, because they can lead us to unexpected discoveries and unique experiences. The yellow light represents the imperfection in us and also where the unexpected discovery lives. It's the place where our compassion, empathy, fear, and desire all collide at a single intersection.

In your life, a yellow light might be a decision to move across the country with your family and change careers by working at a tech startup, like I did. It might be leaving a safe, well-paid position to step into the unknown. It might be helping a friend or colleague rise to their highest self and greatest potential. It could be deciding whether to have a child, or taking the risk of telling someone you love them for the first time.

The yellow light is where the risk is high and where the greatest potential dwells. It's where boundaries are only semi-formed and thus can allow us to discover and grow exponentially. However, just like driving, you must proceed with caution. Caution in this case doesn't mean fear. It means paying attention to the present moment, seeing things clearly for what they are, and then choosing to step onto the path.

Songlines: The Songs We Inherit

Aboriginal Australians navigate their continent through song. Over countless generations, they've woven their knowledge of the land into melodies that serve as both map and memory. These Songlines aren't written down or drawn on paper. They live in the voices of those who sing them, passed from elder to child in an unbroken chain stretching back through history to what they call the Dreamtime.

We carry our own songlines, though we rarely recognize them as such. Our families and cultures have been singing to us since before we could speak. They've taught us what matters, what threatens, what success looks like, where safety lies. These songs shape how we read every landscape we encounter.

Consider the melodies you mapped growing up without consciously realizing it. Perhaps your family sang variations on the theme of academic achievement, each verse reinforcing how good grades open doors that lead to security. Or maybe your cultural tradition hummed warnings about straying too far from home, celebrating those who stayed close while mourning those who left. Some of us inherited songs about accumulating resources, others about distributing them. Some learned harmonies of rigid roles, others of fluid self-creation.

The executive who can't stop checking email at midnight isn't just dedicated to her job. She's following a songline that equates rest with laziness, worth with output. The entrepreneur who bets everything on an untested idea might be singing a family ballad about pioneers and risk-takers, where security plays the villain's role.

Most of us don't know we're singing. We think we're making rational choices based on a clear-eyed assessment of reality. But we're actually following melodic paths laid down so early we can't remember learning them. The verse about "never show them you're struggling" feels like universal truth, not one possible tune among infinite others.

Writing Your Own Songline

Language is one of the primary codes we use to program our consciousness. Every story we tell ourselves, every description we give to our experiences, becomes part of the operating system that guides our decisions and shapes our perception. But these linguistic maps often remain disconnected from our bodies, floating as abstract concepts rather than lived truth.

The practice of writing your own songline creates a bridge between inherited patterns and conscious choice. First, you identify the songs you received. What did your family sing about money? About conflict? About rest? About success? About love? These aren't questions you answer once. They reveal themselves over time as you notice your automatic responses to different situations.

Once you can hear the inherited melodies, you can begin composing new ones. This isn't about rejecting everything you learned. Some inherited songs serve you well. The question is whether you're singing them by choice or by default.

The songline practice uses the simple act of walking through a meaningful place while speaking your observations aloud. Take a walk through a familiar physical space and begin describing what you notice. Use your senses to take in the environment. Is there a quality to the moisture of the air, visual landmarks that reach out to you, or a fragrance that catches your attention? Use that walk to connect with your feelings, memories, and moments that you experienced in the culture you came from and the one you are creating. See them intersecting in the land and sky.

One of my favorite songlines is being out just before dawn on the Lower East Side of New York and walking by a multigenerational family run bakery that's just finishing their first round of baking for the day. This bakery was amazing because if you were local, you knew you could go to their side door and buy bread fresh from the oven before they had opened to the public. Remembering that place as I write this story brings back moments of deep connection from long nights with dear friends and nourishment on the way home in the morning to rest before the start of the day. Every time I think of it, it brings joy to my heart.

We are writing songlines all the time. The more we can bring them into our conscious mind as we're doing it, the more present we become, the clearer the world is around us, and the more we get to see how we're encoding our perception. Once we can see that encoding, it becomes much easier to find the points of change that we want to make. This is a map that captures what we know in our bones and tells the story of where we've been and helps us orient ourselves to where we are going.

Three Pillars of Effective Boundaries

Through years of working with individuals across industries, I've identified three essential pillars that determine whether boundaries will guide growth or simply restrict it.

Clarity. Effective boundaries must be clearly defined, create meaningful results, and be understood by all. Ambiguity creates confusion, not freedom. The boundaries between you and others, between appropriate and inappropriate, between what's negotiable and what isn't, all must be articulated with precision.

Congruence. Your boundaries must align with your core values and authentic self. Incongruent boundaries, those adopted from others or maintained out of obligation rather than conviction, create internal conflict rather than channeling energy productively.

Flexibility. Boundaries shouldn't be rigid fortresses but permeable membranes that adapt to changing conditions. Like a river that adjusts its flow around obstacles, effective boundaries respond to new information and evolving circumstances.

Through a boundary audit, a senior executive I worked with discovered that her boundary of "always being available to the team" was actually undermining both her effectiveness and her team's growth. By redesigning this boundary to create protected time for deep work and strategic thinking, she not only improved her own performance but also empowered her team to develop greater problem-solving capabilities.

The Boundary Ecosystem

Boundaries exist not in isolation but as part of complex systems that interact with and influence each other. This ecological understanding is vital for leaders navigating multi-layered organizations. Just as a river's impact extends far beyond its banks, creating microhabitats, responding to weather patterns, and shaping the landscape, our boundaries affect far more than just our immediate interactions.

To map your boundary ecosystem, start by identifying the major areas of your life or organization where boundaries operate: work processes, team relationships, client interactions, time with family, self-care, fitness, and creativity. For each system, identify the primary boundaries that define how it operates. Then trace connections between boundaries that influence each other. Some boundaries reinforce each other. Some conflict.

Look for leverage points in boundaries that if adjusted, would create positive ripple effects throughout multiple systems. This visual mapping process reveals the hidden connections between seemingly separate parts of your life or organization, allowing for more strategic boundary setting that considers the entire ecosystem rather than isolated elements.

The Dynamic Nature of Boundaries

Remember, boundaries give shape to our lives. They help us understand contexts where we begin and end, how we relate to others, and how we move through the world. But boundaries are not fixed. They are dynamic, constantly evolving as we grow and change. Just as rivers carve their way through mountains, creating new paths and ecosystems along the way, we too must navigate the boundaries of our lives with a sense of adaptability and flow.

The most effective boundaries evolve through three distinct phases.

Formation. When boundaries are first established, they often need to be relatively rigid as we develop new patterns. Like the initial carving of a river channel, this phase may require focused effort and clear definition.

Integration. As boundaries become familiar, they begin to integrate with our natural way of being. The effort required to maintain them decreases as they become part of our identity and operating system.

Evolution. Mature boundaries adapt to new circumstances and insights. Rather than becoming obsolete or calcified, they remain responsive to our growth and changing environments.

Consider how this applies to a leader implementing a new communication practice like OKRs (Objectives and Key Results) within their team. Initially, the boundary requires explicit reinforcement and reminders. As team members integrate the new expectations, the boundary becomes part of the team's culture. Eventually, the boundary evolves to accommodate unique situations while maintaining its essential purpose.

When we understand the nature of boundaries as opportunities for growth rather than rigid barriers, we can approach the journey ahead with ease and confidence. Whether the light is red, green, or yellow, we can trust in our ability to move or be still, shaping and being shaped by the boundaries we create and encounter as we walk along our path.

Practice: Personal Boundary Mapping

Applied Insights

The capacity to see your boundaries as channels that direct energy rather than walls that restrict it. This practice trains you to identify where your boundaries are clear and serving you, where they're absent and energy is leaking, and where they're evolving in the yellow-light zone of growth. Over time, you develop the ability to create boundaries that liberate rather than limit.

When to Use

- When you feel consistently drained without clear cause
- When others regularly overstep and you can't seem to stop it
- When you sense energy leaking but don't know where
- When entering a new role, relationship, or life phase
- When a boundary that once served you now feels restrictive
- As a periodic life audit to catch drift before it becomes a problem

The Practice

This practice is not about a single situation. It's an audit across your life, surveying where your boundaries are clear and serving you, where they're not serving you; where they're absent, and energy is leaking, and where they're evolving in the yellow-light zone of growth.

You'll scan multiple domains as you move through the phases. Let the practice reveal where your attention is most needed rather than deciding in advance.

Phase One: Embodied Strength

Before thinking about boundaries, feel your own strength.

Sit upright in a chair with your spine erect. Press your feet firmly into the ground, feeling the tension rise through your legs. With your arms at your sides, make fists with your hands at about fifty percent of your strength, tight enough to feel your forearms activate. Press your shoulders down toward your hips, creating tension through your arms and upper back. Press the crown of your head up toward the sky, lengthening your neck.

Hold this integrated tension throughout your body. You're not straining. You're activating. Feel yourself as a unified system of strength.

This physical strength parallels the strength of your intent. Boundaries require the same quality: engaged, clear, directed, and flexible. Weakness in the body mirrors weakness in boundaries. Strength in the body supports strength in commitment.

Release most of the tension so that your body feels activated, upright, and relaxed.

From this activated state, bring to mind different areas of your life: your work, your primary relationships, your health, your creative life, your finances. As you hold each area in mind, notice your body's response. Where does the tension hold steady? Where does it waver or want to collapse? Where does discomfort arise?

Steady strength often signals boundaries that are working. Wavering or discomfort often signals boundaries that are absent, violated, or unclear.

Note which areas created the strongest response. Release the tension, take a breath, and continue.

Phase Two: The Three Categories

On your paper, create three columns: Clear, Absent, and Evolving.

Clear Boundaries: Where do you know exactly what you will and won't do? Where do others respect your limits without constant enforcement? Where does your energy flow productively? List what's working. Name the specific boundary, not just the domain. "I don't check email after 8 p.m." rather than just "work."

Absent Boundaries: Where do you consistently feel drained? Where do others overstep regularly? Where can you not seem to say no? These are the areas where your tension wavered or collapsed in Phase One. List what's missing or leaking. Be specific. "I say yes to every request for my time from my team" rather than just "work boundaries."

Evolving Boundaries: Where are you in the yellow-light zone? These are boundaries in transition. New roles where you're still defining your approach, relationships where the rules are shifting, creative projects pushing you beyond familiar territory. These aren't problems. They're growth edges. List what's actively evolving.

Phase Three: The Constraint Gift

Choose one item from your Absent column, a place where you're leaking energy, progress, or clarity.

Now consider: if this boundary were firmly in place, what would it force you to do differently? What creative solution might emerge from the constraint?

Remember Dr. Seuss writing *Green Eggs and Ham* with only fifty words. The constraint didn't limit his creativity. It channeled it into something more powerful than open-ended freedom would have produced.

Answer the question: If I held this boundary, what would I have to change?

Often the "have to" reveals the gift. You'd have to delegate. You'd have to prioritize. You'd have to ask for help. You'd have to disappoint someone, and that would be ok because of the potential for a more aligned outcome.

Phase Four: One Boundary, One Week

From your Absent column, choose one boundary to establish or strengthen this week. Choose something significant enough to matter but contained enough to actually hold.

Write the boundary in clear language. Not "better work-life balance" but "I will leave the office by 6pm on Tuesday and Thursday no matter what." Not "more time for myself" but "I will take a walk alone for twenty minutes every morning before checking my phone."

Effective boundaries have three pillars:

Clarity: Anyone hearing it would know exactly what it means.

Congruence: It aligns with your values, not outside expectations.

Flexibility: It can adapt to unusual circumstances without collapsing entirely.

Test your boundary against these three. Revise until it passes.

Results will show the impact of your actions. If they aren't aligned with your expectations, reassess.

Adaptations

Quick version (10 minutes): Skip to Phase Four. Identify one boundary that's absent or leaking. Write it clearly. Tell one person today.

Deep version (60+ minutes): Expand Phase Two into a full life audit. Map every significant domain. Journal about the history of your boundary patterns. Where did you learn them? Which ones are inherited and no longer fit?

Partner version: Do the practice with someone you trust. Share your three columns. Ask them what boundaries they see you struggling with that you might not recognize. Others often see our leaks before we do.

Quarterly review: Return to this practice every three months. Boundaries need maintenance. What was clear may have drifted. What was evolving may have solidified. What was absent may have been addressed or may have gotten worse.

What to Expect

First few times: You may struggle to distinguish between boundaries that serve you and boundaries you've inherited without examination. The embodied strength scan helps here. Your body knows the difference even when your mind is confused. You may also feel resistance to naming absent boundaries because doing so implies you need to change something.

After a few times of doing the practice: You'll start recognizing boundary violations in real-time rather than after you're already drained. The language of clear, absent, and evolving becomes a quick diagnostic you can run mentally. You'll notice that strong boundaries actually improve relationships rather than damaging them.

Common Obstacles

"If I set this boundary, I'll disappoint people." Yes. Boundaries disappoint people who benefited from their absence. This isn't cruelty. It's clarity. The disappointment is often briefer and less damaging than you fear. And the alignment you create serves everyone over time.

"My situation is too complicated for clear boundaries." Complex situations need more boundaries, not less. Start smaller. You don't have to solve everything at once. One clear boundary in one domain creates ripple effects. Complexity is often the excuse we use to avoid the discomfort of change.

Field Note

Adrian was someone who always responded to whatever was put in front of him. If someone asked him to do something, he'd do it. He was running a team responsible for roadmap execution, client communication, and product implementation. He was working fourteen-hour days and still never had time to get everything done.

When he sat down to examine his boundaries, I had him start with his body. Where did his strength hold steady, and where did it waver? The moment he brought his team to mind, his shoulders collapsed forward. His body already knew what his mind was avoiding.

What emerged was this: his attachment to being of service was getting in the way of saying no. His overdeveloped sense of responsibility kept him from delegating. Every time a team member hit a problem, Adrian stepped in to solve it.

The question became: If Adrian created protected focus time, what would happen? He wouldn't be available to help his team work through certain problems. They'd have to attempt solutions on their own.

When he implemented the boundary, there was friction. A team member came to his office during focus time, saw the closed door, and sent a frustrated Slack message. Adrian held the line. By the end of the first week, something shifted. Problems that used to land on his desk were getting solved without him.

Within a month, the team was operating at a level Adrian hadn't seen before. The constraint he'd been afraid to set had created exactly the space his team needed to grow.

Remember This

Boundaries are not walls that imprison us but riverbanks that give our energy direction and power. Like the relationship between river and mountain, where neither force compromises its essential nature yet together they create fertile valleys and thriving ecosystems, our boundaries enable growth rather than restrict our highest potential.

The yellow light moments in our lives, those uncertain spaces between stop and go, are not obstacles to avoid but invitations to growth. They represent the imperfection that makes us unique, the place where our compassion, empathy, fear, and desire collide at a single intersection. When we proceed through these moments with conscious awareness rather than automatic reaction, we discover possibilities that rigid red-and-green thinking would never reveal.

We carry songlines inherited from our families and cultures, melodic patterns that shape how we navigate every landscape we encounter. Most of us don't know we're singing. The practice is learning to hear the inherited songs, keeping what serves us, and composing new verses that align with who we're becoming.

Clear boundaries create freedom precisely because they eliminate the constant negotiation of undefined spaces. When everyone understands the agreements, movement becomes almost effortless. The key is developing the awareness to recognize when boundaries are serving as guides toward growth and when they've become barriers to your next evolution.

7

FINDING FLOW

"Let your life lightly dance on the edges of Time
like dew on the tip of a leaf."
— Rabindranath Tagore

In 1989, I was twenty-five and convinced I understood how effort worked. If something didn't come naturally, you just applied more force. In martial arts that meant tightening everything: shoulders, jaw, breathing, and trying to overpower whoever was in front of me. It wasn't going well. Students kept getting around me, and I couldn't figure out why.

My teacher invited me to meet him for a private session near Boulder Creek. We worked for a few minutes. Same result. I blocked late, reacted late, and moved like I was bracing for impact instead of responding to it. He watched without correcting me, which was somehow worse. Finally, he walked me over to the water.

We stood at the edge for a while. The creek flowed over, under, or around stones and fallen branches with effortless efficiency. The current split, curved, gathered again, and kept going.

"Your movements are like a dam," he said finally, "trying to control and direct everything. They need to be like the water."

That was all.

Back on the grass, I realized I had been forcing a response to a moment that had already changed. When I stopped bracing and let the contact guide my next movement, the timing took care of itself. I wasn't faster or stronger. I was moving naturally from one position to the next, guided by the situation rather than my determination to push through it.

Flow begins once direction and boundaries are clear. Instead of pushing events forward, you let what is happening guide your next action. Movement becomes continuous because you are working with the moment rather than against it.

The Neuroscience of Flow

What I learned that day by the creek would later be confirmed by modern neuroscience. When we enter flow states, our brains undergo remarkable transformations. The prefrontal cortex, our analytical command center, temporarily quiets down. This is the part of our brain that second-guesses, criticizes, and monitors our every move. When it settles down, a kind of spaciousness opens up. We stop watching ourselves and become immersed in the experience.

At the same time, neurochemicals like dopamine, norepinephrine, endorphins, and serotonin cascade through your system, creating a state of heightened focus, creativity, and sense of well-being. Brain activity shifts toward the border between alpha and theta waves, where insight and imagination flourish.

Decades earlier, psychologist Mihaly Csikszentmihalyi identified the universal conditions that trigger flow in individuals and later extended the work to address larger groups. The ingredients for flow are a combination of clear goals, immediate feedback, and the right balance of challenge and skill. Whether you're a surgeon, a musician, or a programmer, these same conditions open the door to the timeless, effortless experience of flow.

In Chapter 4, we explored what happens when you stop doing entirely. When stillness allows insights to surface, that effort cannot force. Flow is different. You're not resting. You're engaged in action. But your inner critic and analytical monitor quiet down in a similar way to what we experience in the later stages of stillness. The result is absorption rather than insight, performance rather than rest. Both states require releasing the grip of effortful thinking. They simply activate that release from different vectors.

Sacred Knowledge Meets Modern Science

The ancient Daoists understood the power of flow intuitively. In the Dao De Jing, water is presented as the highest embodiment of virtue precisely because it demonstrates these qualities naturally: "The highest good is like water. Water gives life to the Ten-Thousand-Things and does not strive. It flows in all places, even those we resist, and so it is like the Dao."

This wisdom, written over two millennia ago, aligns perfectly with our modern understanding of optimal performance and flow states. The Daoists recognized what neuroscience now confirms. Our greatest effectiveness comes not from forcing outcomes through sheer will, but from aligning with natural principles of movement and adaptation.

The Four Elements of Flow Cultivation

Through years of working with leaders, martial artists, athletes, and creatives, four essential elements for cultivating flow in your life and work have emerged: environmental design, mental preparation, physical readiness, and recovery practice. Each of these elements builds upon the others, creating conditions where flow can emerge naturally.

Think of how a skilled gardener creates conditions for plants to thrive. They don't try to force growth. Instead, they prepare the soil, ensure proper drainage, provide appropriate sunlight, and maintain the right balance of nutrients. In the same way, we can create conditions that support our capacity for flow without trying to force the state itself.

Environmental Design: Creating Spaces for Flow

Your physical environment strongly affects your ability to access flow states. Just as water flows differently through various landscapes, your energy and attention move differently through different types of spaces.

One of my clients, a writer struggling with creative blocks, discovered that his sophisticated home office setup was actually preventing flow rather than supporting it. The multiple screens, constant notifications, and even his ergonomic chair were keeping him too comfortable, too connected to the outside world. We simplified his space dramatically, creating what he called his "monk's den." A clean desk, a simple chair, and nothing but the tools he needed for writing.

His productivity was freed up, not because he was trying harder, but because he had created an environment that supported natural flow. The principles we discovered in his case apply broadly. Eliminate unnecessary friction. Remove distractions and interruptions that break your concentration. Create meaningful boundaries. Align your environment with your purpose. Different activities require different environmental conditions.

The key insight is that flow-supporting environments don't need to be perfect or elaborate. They simply need to align with the specific type of flow you're trying to cultivate. Every solution for the boundaries that optimize flow is individual. Through self-awareness, you can discover the best way for you to optimize flow.

I discovered this in my own home, watching the completely different ways my wife Bren and I approach our creative work. When I'm writing or developing new practices, I need some kind of ambient sound, like lo-fi or jazz playing softly. The sound creates a kind of cushion that allows me to resist distraction and focus. Without it, the silence feels thin, and the distractions of mental chatter or things in the room around me instantly pull me out of concentration.

Bren, on the other hand, needs absolute silence when she's writing her memoir. Even the sound of me walking past her office door can pull her out of the deep space where her memories and words connect. "It's like I'm diving into an underwater cave," she explained to me once. "Any sound pulls me back to the surface, and I have to start the dive all over again."

Then there's the matter of visual space. Some creators need to see the horizon while they work. Windows overlooking expansive views that mirror the expansiveness they're trying to access in their creativity. Others do their best work in small, enclosed spaces where the outside world can't intrude, where they can build their own universe without distraction.

These aren't quirks or just preferences. They're essential conditions for each person's creative flow. Knowing which boundaries stimulate and inspire you is critical when designing your creative space. The mistake many of us make is assuming that what works for someone else should work for us, or worse, that there's a "right" way to set up a creative environment. There isn't. There's only what works for you, discovered through patient experimentation and honest self-observation.

Mental Preparation: Clearing the Field

Your mental state before entering flow matters as much as your physical environment. A mind cluttered with unfinished tasks, unprocessed emotions, or ambient anxiety cannot settle into the absorption that flow requires. The noise is too loud.

The most reliable mental preparation I've found is what I call "clearing the field." Before any session where flow would serve you, take five minutes to externalize everything competing for your attention. Write down the tasks nagging at you. Note the conversation you need to have later. Acknowledge the worry that keeps surfacing. You're not solving these things. You're telling your mind that they're captured, that they won't be forgotten, that you can return to them after.

This works because your brain's open loops consume cognitive resources. Each unfinished task or unresolved concern takes up working memory, leaving less available for the complete immersion that flow requires. By externalizing them, you close the loops temporarily. Your mind can let go.

A product designer I worked with had struggled with flow for months. She'd sit down to work and find herself checking email, scrolling through Slack, unable to settle. When we examined her mental state before work sessions, she realized she was carrying a constant background hum of anxiety about things she might be forgetting. We introduced a simple ritual: before any design session, she'd spend three minutes writing every open loop onto a single index card. The card sat face-down on her desk. She didn't look at it during the session. But knowing it existed, knowing nothing would slip through the cracks, freed her attention to dive deep.

Within two weeks, she was accessing a level of flow she hadn't experienced for a long time.

The ritual itself becomes a signal. Just as athletes have pre-game routines that shift their nervous system into performance mode, your mental preparation ritual tells your brain and body that it's time to transition. The content of the ritual matters less than its consistency. Some people journal for five minutes. Some review their intentions for the session. Some simply sit in silence and breathe until the mental chatter settles. Pay attention to what works for you. That's what you'll naturally do anyway. Repeat it until your brain recognizes the pattern and begins the shift automatically. Remember, you do this all the time already without it being conscious. We are just making it intentional.

Physical Readiness: The Body's Role in Flow

Physical readiness connects directly to what we discussed in Chapter 1 about body listening and awareness. Our bodies have natural rhythms of energy and recovery, peaks and valleys of alertness and rest. Learning to read and respect these rhythms is crucial for accessing flow states reliably.

One executive I worked with discovered that his best strategic thinking happened not during his scheduled morning meetings, but in the quiet hours of late afternoon when his body was naturally more relaxed and his mind more open to creative insights. For years, he had been forcing deep work into morning slots because that's when productivity experts said he should do it. By restructuring his schedule to align with his actual rhythms, he dramatically improved both the quality of his decisions and his enjoyment of the process.

Physical readiness also involves understanding the role of tension and relaxation in flow. As we mentioned earlier: Too much tension blocks flow. Too little provides insufficient structure for directed energy. The ideal state is what Qigong practitioners call "relaxed readiness." Alert but not tense. Focused but not rigid.

Your body sends clear signals about its readiness for flow. Shallow breathing, tight shoulders, or a clenched jaw all indicate a system too activated to settle into absorption. Sluggishness, foggy thinking, or heaviness suggest a system that needs movement or rest before it can engage. The practice is learning to read these signals honestly rather than overriding them with caffeine or willpower.

A simple physical reset can shift your state quickly. Before a session where you want to access flow, take two minutes to move. Shake out your arms and legs. Roll your shoulders. Take five deep breaths with extended exhales. This isn't elaborate preparation. It's simply giving your body what it needs to arrive in a state where flow becomes possible.

Recovery: The Forgotten Element of Flow

Recovery practice is perhaps the most overlooked aspect of flow cultivation, yet it's absolutely essential. Flow states are enormously demanding on your system, requiring significant energy and resources. Without proper recovery, our capacity for flow diminishes over time. We'll explore this more deeply in the Rhythm of Life chapter.

Think of it this way. Recovery isn't just about getting enough sleep, muscle recovery, or taking breaks. It's about creating intentional practices that help us integrate the experiences and learning that occur during flow states.

I learned this lesson the hard way early in my practice. I would often find myself in such deep states of flow while working with clients that I would schedule sessions back-to-back, riding the wave of engagement and puzzle-solving. Eventually, this led to a kind of flow state burnout. I had the skill to access the state but hadn't developed the wisdom to balance it with recovery.

Now I build in "integration intervals" between sessions. Short periods where I can fully absorb and process what occurred before moving on. This practice connects directly to what we will look at in the chapter on renewal. The need for recovery is an essential element of sustainable high performance.

The ratio matters. For every period of deep flow, you need corresponding recovery. This doesn't mean equal time. A ninety-minute flow session might need only fifteen minutes of integration. But skipping recovery entirely, stacking flow sessions or context switching straight into another activity, depletes resources that take a long time to rebuild.

Flow Triggers and Rituals

Researchers and practitioners in the flow space have identified something interesting about how we can deliberately create conditions for flow. They've identified what they call "environmental flow triggers." Specific elements that, when present, dramatically increase our chances of entering that coveted state.

Think of these triggers as the ingredients in a recipe. Clear goals that give us direction. A challenge that matches our skill level. Not so easy we're bored, not so hard we're anxious. Immediate feedback that lets us know how we're doing moment by moment.

But here's what makes it interesting. When we consistently experience these triggers in the same environment, something alchemical happens. Our brains begin to associate that specific place or routine with the flow state itself. This is the power of ritual. Those repetitive behaviors that signal to our consciousness that we're shifting from one state to another.

Think about any ritual you've witnessed or participated in. Whether it's a tea ceremony, a pre-game warmup, or even your morning coffee routine, rituals work because they create a bridge between states of being. The repetitive nature of the ritual tells our nervous system what's coming next. It's like sending an advance team to prepare the terrain. By the time you arrive at your destination, everything is already set up and waiting for you.

When I wrote the first draft of this book, I went into my office on Saturday and Sunday mornings and committed to writing a minimum of 2000 words per day. At first, what was a difficult task became almost automatic. I would step into my empty office on the weekends with its quiet hum of air conditioning and the slight buzz of computers, and the words would pour onto the page.

When we create rituals around our flow practice, we're essentially training our brains to recognize the signals and respond accordingly. The ritual becomes a form of communication with our deeper selves, saying "This is the time, this is the place, this is what we're doing now." Our intent becomes focused, our perception shifts, and our entire relationship with the environment transforms. What was once just a desk becomes a sacred space for creation. What was once just background music becomes the soundtrack to peak performance.

These "flow anchors" work because repetition is how we reinforce and grow neural pathways. Each time we perform our ritual and enter flow, we strengthen the association. Eventually, the ritual itself becomes so powerful that it can pull us into flow even on days when we're feeling scattered or resistant. The environment and the ritual together become allies in our quest for that state where everything clicks and time seems to fall away.

The Evolutionary Purpose of Flow

From an evolutionary perspective, flow states have a clear adaptive advantage. When our ancestors needed to track prey, respond to predators, or navigate complex social dynamics, the heightened perception and performance of flow would have provided a significant edge.

This evolutionary heritage explains why flow states are associated with activities that mirror ancestral challenges. Physical movement, strategic thinking, creative problem-solving, and deep social connection. These are precisely the areas where our species needed to excel in order to thrive.

Understanding this evolutionary background helps explain why certain activities seem to trigger flow more readily than others. Activities that combine physical engagement, skill development, immediate feedback, and clear goals tap into these ancient pathways, activating flow states more readily.

This perspective connects directly to what we explored in chapter 5. How our evolutionary heritage provides a foundation for adaptation and effectiveness in the modern world.

The Integration Journey

The ultimate goal isn't to experience occasional flow states but to develop "flow capacity." The ability to move easily between different states of consciousness as appropriate to the situation. Sometimes we need the analytical focus of the prefrontal cortex. Other times we need the creative absorption of flow.

Like the water in our mountain stream, we develop the wisdom to know when to flow swiftly and when to pool deeply, when to carve new channels and when to follow existing paths. This capacity doesn't develop overnight, but through consistent practice and awareness.

Remember that like water, flow cannot be forced. It can only be allowed. Your task is not to create flow but to remove the obstacles that prevent it. As the Daoists remind us: "Nature does not hurry, yet everything is accomplished." This wisdom applies perfectly to the cultivation of flow states.

The journey to mastering flow is itself a practice in flowing. Some days you'll find yourself in deep states of absorption and effectiveness. On other days, you'll feel blocked and restricted. The key is to approach both experiences with the adaptability of water. Neither attaching to the easy moments nor resisting the challenging ones.

Through consistent practice and patient observation, you'll develop "Water Wisdom." The ability to navigate and adapt with grace, power, and effectiveness. Like the mountain stream that highlighted my own understanding, you'll learn to navigate life's obstacles not through force but through flowing intelligence.

Practice: The Four Elements of Flow

Applied Insights

The capacity to create conditions where flow becomes accessible rather than accidental. This practice trains you to assess and strengthen the four elements that support sustained, effortless performance: your environment, your mental state, your physical readiness, and your recovery rhythms. Over time, you develop a reliable system for entering flow when you need it.

When to Use

- When you want to increase the frequency of flow experiences
- When flow used to come easily but now feels elusive
- As a periodic audit to maintain your flow capacity
- When preparing for a period of intensive creative or strategic work

The Practice

Find 20-30 minutes of quiet space with paper or a journal. This practice is not about a single question or challenge. It's about creating conditions where flow becomes accessible rather than accidental.

You'll assess four elements that support sustained performance: your environment, your mental state, your physical readiness, and your recovery rhythms. The goal is to identify what's working, find your weak link, and design a simple ritual that helps you enter flow more reliably.

Phase One: Flow Memory

Before analyzing, remember.

Close your eyes. Recall a recent time when you were in flow. Not just productive but genuinely absorbed. Time has disappeared. Effort felt effortless. You and the work merged.

If no recent memory comes, reach further back. Everyone has experienced flow at some point, even if it was years ago.

Once you have the memory, step into it fully. Where were you? What time of day was it? What were the conditions around you? What had you done to prepare? How did your body feel? What happened afterward? If you can remember a few of these moments, it helps create more flow anchors.

Open your eyes and write brief notes, capturing the details. These notes contain your personal flow fingerprint. Remember, what works for you is unique to you.

Phase Two: The Four Elements Assessment

Using your flow memory as a reference point, assess each element honestly.

Environment: Where do you work best? What conditions support your focus? Consider sound (silence, music, ambient noise), visual field (cluttered, minimal, natural light), tools within reach, and interruption patterns. Compare your ideal environment to your current one. Either shift environments or make some changes that will allow the one you're in to align more with a flow space.

Mental Preparation: How do you prepare your mind for deep work? Do you have rituals that signal transition into focus? Methods for clearing mental clutter? Ways of setting intention? Or do you simply dive in and hope for the best? Notice the ones that are most effective.

Physical Readiness: What state is your body in when you attempt focused work? Consider sleep quality, energy levels, physical tension, and whether you've moved your body recently. Your mind reflects your physical state. A depleted body cannot sustain flow. Rate your typical physical readiness from one to ten.

Recovery: How do you restore after periods of intense focus? Do you have practices for integration and rest? Or do you push until depletion and then crash? Flow without recovery leads to burnout. Rate your recovery practices from one to ten.

Phase Three: Finding the Weak Link

Look at your four elements for flow. Which area was the least developed? This is your weak link; the element most likely to prevent flow even when the others are strong.

Every chain breaks at its weakest link. You can have a perfect environment, strong mental preparation, and good physical readiness, but if you never recover, the system eventually fails. You can be well-rested and mentally clear, but if your environment invites constant interruption, flow cannot take hold.

Write your weak link element at the top of a fresh page.

Below it, answer: How can I re-design this element to optimize stepping into flow? Be specific. Not "A better environment" but "noise-canceling headphones, or the phone in another room; my door closed from 9am to noon."

Phase Four: The Flow Ritual

Flow responds to ritual. When you consistently perform certain actions before entering flow, your brain recognizes them and automatically gets ready to step into flow. The ritual becomes the trigger.

Design a brief flow ritual that touches all four elements.

Environment: One action to prepare your space. Clear the desk. Close unnecessary tabs. Put the phone away. Adjust lighting.

Mental: One action to signal transition. Three breaths. Review your intention for the session. Read a quote that centers you. A moment of stillness. A fresh cup of coffee.

Physical: One action to prepare your body. Stand and stretch. Roll your shoulders. Drink water. Feel your feet on the ground.

Recovery cue: Set a timer or note that reminds you to take a break. Ninety minutes is a natural focus cycle and a good place to start for most people. Knowing the end point helps you commit fully to the beginning.

Write out your ritual in order. Keep it simple enough that you'll actually do it. It should fit on a post-it. Put it on the wall in front of your workspace.

Phase Five: The First Test

Commit to using your ritual before your next work session that requires deep focus.

Before you begin, rate your expectation of entering flow from one to ten. After the session, rate what actually happened. Track this over your next five focused work sessions.

This data tells you whether your ritual is working or needs adjustment. Flow practice is experimental. What works on paper may need refinement in reality.

Pay attention to the frequency and accessibility to flow. This is how you measure the impact. If it's not aligned, reassess.

Adaptations

Quick version (10 minutes): Skip to Phase Three. Identify your weakest element. Write one specific improvement. Implement it today.

Deep version (60+ minutes): Expand Phase Two into a full audit. For each element, map your history. When has this element been strong? When has it failed you? What patterns emerge? Journal about your relationship with each element.

Environment sprint: Spend some time going deep to optimize your physical workspace. Remove everything unnecessary. Change the furniture arrangement to create a new viewpoint. Add what's missing. Create a space that invites focus and creativity.

Recovery focus: If recovery is your weak link, design a post-flow ritual as carefully as your pre-flow ritual. Movement, hydration, a brief walk, journaling what emerged. Make completion as intentional as beginning. Your brain needs to recover. We do this by changing our activity and focus.

What to Expect

First few times: The ritual may feel artificial or forced. You may forget steps or rush through them. Flow may not arrive on command. This is normal. You're building new patterns. The ritual's power comes from repetition, not from perfection on day one.

After a few times of doing the practice: The ritual begins to work automatically. Your body recognizes the cues and starts shifting toward focus before you consciously direct it. You'll notice flow arriving more reliably. You'll also notice more quickly when an element is off and needs attention.

Common Obstacles

"I don't have control over my environment." Work with what you can control. Headphones create an auditory environment even in open offices. A consistent object on your desk can serve as a visual anchor. Small rituals signal your brain even when you can't change the larger space. Control what you can and accept what you can't.

"I don't have time for rituals." Five minutes of preparation often saves an hour of scattered effort. The question isn't whether you have time for a ritual. The question is whether you can afford the cost of entering important work without one. Start with a sixty-second version if needed.

Field Note

It took me a while to understand my flow in writing because it had changed over time. Originally, I liked to write in quiet spaces with a good view of nature from a window. But with this book, I ended up spending weekends in my office when no one was there, walking the hallway and dictating the first draft. I would set specific goals of 2000 words per session, two sessions per week, and that got me to the first draft.

I needed to be in motion to stimulate my thinking. I do my best thinking when I'm walking and swimming, and I needed a way to record it. An empty environment with no distractions and enough space for me to move turned out to be the best way for me to access my creativity.

After each walking session, I would sit down and edit what I'd dictated until it was clear. That last piece was important because the ideas were fresh but needed to be transformed into clean text.

I never would have expected that pacing my empty office on weekend mornings was how I would write this book. But when I was honest about the environment I needed and how my flow state was activated, the path to writing it was easy and fun. I looked forward to every weekend when I would get to dive back in.

Remember This

Flow cannot be forced. It can only be allowed. Your task is not to create flow but to remove the obstacles that prevent it.

The four elements work together like a garden's ecosystem: environmental design, mental preparation, physical readiness, and recovery practice. Each element supports the others. Neglect one, and the system eventually fails.

Your flow conditions are personal. What works for someone else may not work for you. The writer who needs silence and the one who needs ambient sound are both right. Discovery comes through patient experimentation and honest self-observation.

Rituals become triggers. When you consistently perform certain actions before entering flow, your brain learns the pattern. Eventually, the ritual itself can pull you into flow even on days when you're feeling scattered. The environment and the ritual together become allies in accessing your best work.

8

THE PERCEPTION GAP

"We do not see things as they are; we see them as we are."
— Anonymous

I was teaching a martial arts class at our Tribeca studio. One of my more talented students, Sarah, was working on a technique she had been practicing for months. But that day, something was off. She kept trying the same move over and over, each attempt making her more frustrated than the last.

"I can't get this right," she finally said, shaking her head.

I had been watching her, and what I saw was completely different from what she was experiencing. Her form was actually quite good. Not perfect, but certainly not the disaster she was describing.

"Sarah, come here for a second," I said. "Watch Ian do it."

Ian, another student, demonstrated the technique. Sarah watched intently, then described what she saw: the fluid movement, the natural flow from one position to the next. She could see it clearly in someone else.

"Ok," I said, pulling out my phone. "Now watch this."

I showed her a video I had taken just ten minutes earlier of her performing the exact same technique. The movement was smooth, controlled, and flawless.

She stared at the phone with confusion. "But that's not what it feels like while I'm doing it," she said. "When I'm doing it, I feel stiff and clumsy."

The gap between what we experience and what is actually happening can be enormous. Sarah genuinely felt like she was moving one way, but the reality captured on video told a completely different story. How we experience something and how others experience it is rarely in perfect alignment.

Imagine being in the desert. You think you see a lake shimmering in the distance. The mirage feels absolutely real. You are sure it is water. You get thirsty, and that reinforces the belief. You desperately hope it is real. Somewhere in the back of your mind, you remember that heat radiating off the ground often shimmers like a lake in the sun, but in the moment, your mind doesn't retrieve that fact. When you get closer, you see it's just more sand.

In our lives, we experience these mirages all the time. We create false perceptions that feel so true we would swear by them. And unlike the desert traveler who eventually discovers the truth, we sometimes never realize we are responding to mirages.

The Architecture of False Perception

In today's world of constant information flow, understanding the difference between mirages and mirrors has become more crucial than ever. Our perception is being shaped by our natural environment, immediate community, and the endless digital information being fed to us by algorithms designed to capture and direct our attention toward advertisements.

Think about the last time you were absolutely certain about something. Perhaps a business decision, a relationship dynamic, or even something as simple as tomorrow's weather. Then you discovered you were completely wrong. These moments of misperception are not failures. They are opportunities to understand how our minds create and maintain our version of reality.

As we explored earlier in the book, our minds are prediction machines evolved to create shortcuts and patterns from limited data. This evolutionary advantage becomes a liability when those predictions go unchecked or when our environment changes faster than our perceptual frameworks can adapt.

The Emptiness of Things

Think of a pencil.

To a writer, it is a tool for self-expression, a way to capture thoughts before they vanish. To a dog, it is a chew toy. In a survival situation, it becomes a weapon.

Same object. Three completely different realities. The pencil itself is empty of inherent meaning. It does not contain "tool-ness" or "toy-ness" or "weapon-ness." Those meanings are added by the perceiver based on their needs, their history, and their context.

This is what contemplative traditions call emptiness. Not that things do not exist, but that they do not carry fixed, built-in meaning. The meaning we experience is not in the object. It is in the relationship between the object and the one perceiving it.

This applies to everything. A delayed email. A glance from a colleague. A quarterly result. A comment from your partner. None of these carry inherent meaning. They are empty until we fill them with interpretation.

The question becomes: How do we fill that emptiness? What mechanism turns neutral facts into the charged experiences we have? Understanding this process is the first step toward seeing our mirages for what they are.

The Five Skandhas: Layers of Construction

Eastern traditions have long understood this challenge. The Heart Sutra, a fundamental Buddhist text, offers us the concept of the Five Skandhas or "heaps." This is a practical framework for understanding how we process and interpret reality. What is fascinating is how closely this ancient view aligns with neuroscience's understanding of perception and consciousness.

The Five Skandhas describe how we move from raw experience to the world of our perceptions:

Form (Rupa): The tangible, physical aspect of experience

Sensation (Vedana): The immediate feeling tone, either pleasant, unpleasant, or neutral

Perception (Samjna): The recognition and interpretation of what we are experiencing

Mental Formations (Samskara): The thoughts, intentions, and mental factors that arise

Consciousness (Vijnana): The awareness that knows all of the above

Let me show you how these create our reality through something we've all experienced. I was living in New York City when the governor announced the pandemic shutdown in March 2020. Within hours, something shifted in the collective consciousness of millions of New Yorkers. We had gone from a city that never sleeps to one that did not know if it would wake up tomorrow.

I remember walking to a local supermarket that evening. The shelves that had been full that morning were stripped bare. No toilet paper, no hand sanitizer, no pasta, no canned goods. People were loading shopping carts like they were preparing for a siege. A woman next to me had four packages of paper towels in her arms, tears in her eyes. "I don't even know why I'm buying these," she said. "I just feel like I have to."

This was our collective mirage. We believed that civilization was about to collapse, that supply chains would fail completely, that we needed to hoard to survive. Let us look at this through the Five Skandhas:

Form: The tangible reality was that stores had temporary shortages, but supply chains were not destroyed. There was just a shift occurring that we had never seen before. Food was still being produced and delivered, just not in the same patterns. That change in form caused us to shift our sensations.

Sensation: Our immediate response was fear. We felt the sensation of a tight chest when seeing empty shelves, the physical tension of uncertainty, and all the sympathetic responses of imminent danger.

Perception: We interpreted our fear and physical sensations through our existing frameworks. Empty shelves meant danger; masks meant contagion everywhere, distance meant isolation.

Mental Formations: From these perceptions elaborate thought constructions arose. We created mental models of societal collapse, imagined scenarios of running out of food, and many of us built justifications for hoarding.

Consciousness: Our awareness became completely absorbed in this constructed reality, unable to see it as only one possible interpretation among many.

What makes this example so powerful is how differently it played out across the country. Friends in rural Montana told me they felt like they were watching a movie about a parallel universe. Some communities saw it as an overblown city problem, others as a government conspiracy, still others as nature's way of forcing us to slow down. Same virus, same pandemic, but completely different perceptions based on where you stood.

Common Perceptual Patterns

Through years of working with leaders across diverse organizations, I have identified recurring patterns in how we create false perceptions. Each of us has characteristic perceptual patterns. These are habitual ways of seeing and interpreting our experience. These patterns act like filters, screening out certain information while highlighting others. Identifying your base habitual patterns is the first step toward more conscious perception.

The Catastrophizer tends to see the worst possible outcome in ambiguous situations. This leader interprets a delayed email as a sign the deal is falling apart, a quiet meeting as evidence the team is disengaged, a market dip as the beginning of a larger downturn.

The Rationalizer quickly develops intellectual explanations that may miss emotional realities. They will create elaborate logical frameworks for why the team is underperforming while completely missing that people feel unheard or undervalued.

The Personalizer interprets events as specifically directed toward or about oneself. When the board asks tough questions, they assume it is because they have lost confidence specifically in them, rather than recognizing that the board asks tough questions of everyone in order to surface the best path forward.

The Generalizer extrapolates specific incidents into universal patterns. One difficult client becomes "clients are impossible," one failed initiative becomes "innovation doesn't work here," one piece of critical feedback becomes "I'm not cut out for this."

The Polarizer sees situations in black and white terms without recognizing nuance. People are either allies or enemies, strategies are either perfect or worthless, outcomes are either triumph or disaster.

These archetypes do not tell the whole story. But they do identify behavioral trends that tend to show up as personality shortcuts we unconsciously use in different situations. They are not inherently right or wrong. They are effective strategies we have built to make sense of complex information quickly. The problem arises when we are unaware of these patterns and fail to recognize how they shape our perception. When we are conscious of these patterns, we can then choose to engage with them or notice when they are clouding our judgment.

The Bias Blind Spot

Emily Pronin, social psychologist at Princeton University, published research on the bias blind spot, revealing another layer of how we create false perceptions. Her study demonstrates that while we are much better at recognizing cognitive biases in others, we struggle to spot them in ourselves. Even when people are explicitly taught about perceptual biases, they typically rate themselves as less susceptible than average, which is of course a blind spot."

This research highlights why systematic practices for examining our perceptions are so important. Without structured approaches, we remain vulnerable to what psychologists call naive realism. This is the belief that we see reality as it truly is, while others who disagree are uninformed, irrational, or biased.

I see this play out regularly in leadership teams. Each executive can clearly see the biases of their colleagues. The CFO's excessive risk aversion, the CMO's over-optimism, and the CTO's tendency to see every problem as a technical challenge. Yet each remains largely blind to their own perceptual filters. It is like we are all walking around with smudged glasses, able to see the smudges on everyone else's lenses but convinced our own are crystal clear. We need each other in order to see these biases. We can't find them by ourselves.

Inherited Perceptual Maps

Our individual perceptions do not exist in isolation. We inherit collective patterns of perception that shape how entire cultures navigate reality. These shared maps can guide us, but they can also trap us in collective mirages that we mistake for fixed reality instead of group delusion.

The songlines we explored in the boundaries chapter are one example of this phenomenon. Those inherited patterns from family and culture shape how we navigate every landscape we encounter. We do not know we are singing. We think we are making rational choices when we are actually following melodic paths laid down so early that we cannot remember learning them. The executive who cannot stop checking email at midnight is not just dedicated to her job. She is following a songline that equates rest with laziness, worth with output. Most of us never examine these inherited maps. They feel like reality itself rather than one possible interpretation among many. Think of a family or cultural perception that you broke out of. What enabled you to shift out of the group perspective?

The Digital Distortion Field

In our hyperconnected world, perceptual challenges have multiplied exponentially. AI-driven social media algorithms, news feeds, and recommendation engines create what I call Digital Distortion Fields. These are environments specifically designed to reinforce our existing beliefs and trigger emotional responses that keep us engaged.

Research from the MIT Media Lab demonstrates that false information spreads six times faster on social networks than accurate information, primarily because it triggers stronger emotional responses. Our perceptual systems, evolved for a world of direct experience, are particularly vulnerable to these digital environments that can amplify and exploit our natural biases.

The technology researcher Linda Stone described this as Continuous Partial Attention. We are never fully engaged with a single reality but constantly processing multiple streams of curated information. Each stream is filtered through algorithms that have learned exactly what will capture our attention, creating personalized mirages that feel completely real.

What is particularly insidious is how these digital distortions reinforce our perceptual patterns. The Catastrophizer's feed fills with worst-case scenarios. The Polarizer sees only content that confirms the world is divided into clear camps. The Personalizer receives a stream of content that seems to speak directly to their specific situation. We think we are seeing reality, but we are actually seeing a carefully curated reflection of our own biases.

Embodied Perception

Our perceptions do not exist solely in our minds. They live in our muscles, our organs, and our cells. Every thought we have, every interpretation we make about our world, creates a cascade of physical responses throughout our body. This is not metaphorical. The field of psychoneuroimmunology has mapped these connections with precision, showing how our perceptions directly alter our biology.

Dr. Antonio Damasio's Somatic Marker Hypothesis reveals that our bodies are constantly creating physical sensations that arise from our accumulated life experiences and help guide our decisions. Every significant experience you have had has left a trace in your body, not just in your memory. That tightening in your chest when you meet someone who reminds you of a person who betrayed you. That warm expansion when you walk into a room that feels like home. These are not random sensations. They are the inner voice of your body's intelligence.

Damasio's research revealed something crucial. Patients with damage to the parts of the brain that process these bodily signals became terrible decision-makers. Even with their logical reasoning intact, they could not navigate complex choices effectively. Without access to their somatic markers, they would spend hours analyzing simple decisions and still make poor choices.

This tells us that these bodily perceptions aren't random or anecdotal feelings or distractions from clear thinking, but rather essential components of it." Our bodies know things our minds haven't figured out yet. That queasy feeling about a business deal might be picking up on subtle cues your analytical mind missed. That sense of expansion and energy around a new opportunity might be recognizing a fit that spreadsheets cannot capture.

Practice: The Perception Audit

Applied Insights

The capacity to recognize when you are seeing a mirage rather than reality. This practice trains you to catch your perceptual patterns in action, deconstruct how you build stories from raw experience, and generate alternative interpretations that may be closer to truth. Over time, you develop the ability to hold your perceptions lightly rather than locking them in a fixed point of view.

When to Use

- When you have had a strong reaction to something and suspect you might not be seeing clearly
- When the same interpretation keeps arising and producing the same unsatisfying results
- After a disagreement, to understand what you might have missed
- When you want to examine an inherited belief that may no longer serve you

The Practice

Find 15-20 minutes of quiet space with paper or a journal. Choose a specific situation where you had a strong reaction, a firm judgment, or any fixed viewpoint that isn't serving you or giving you the results you're looking for.

Phase One: Ground in the Body

Before examining your perception, notice where it lives in your body. Sit comfortably and bring the situation to mind. Do not analyze it. Just let it be present and notice your physical response. Where do you feel tension, heat, or contraction? Chest, jaw, gut, shoulders? What is the quality of your breathing?

Your body holds perceptions before your mind articulates them. This physical signature tells you how charged this situation is and where your system is gripping.

Take five slow breaths, extending the exhale. You are not trying to release the sensation, just creating enough space to observe it clearly.

Phase Two: Identify Your Pattern

Consider if one of the five perceptual patterns might be active in how you are seeing this situation:

Catastrophizer: Seeing the worst possible outcome in ambiguous situations. A delayed response becomes "the deal is falling apart."

Rationalizer: Creating intellectual explanations that miss emotional realities. Building logical frameworks while ignoring that people feel unheard.

Personalizer: Interpreting events as specifically about you. The board's tough questions become evidence they have lost confidence in you specifically.

Generalizer: Extrapolating one incident into universal truth. One difficult client becomes "clients are impossible."

Polarizer: Seeing in black and white without nuance. People are either allies or enemies. Ideas are either brilliant or worthless.

Most of us combine several patterns. Name which one was most dominant in your reaction to this situation.

Phase Three: Layer by Layer

Now deconstruct how you built your perception, using the five layers:

Form: What actually happened? Just the observable facts. "No response to my email for three days" rather than "they're ignoring me." Strip away all interpretation. What would a camera have recorded?

Sensation: What did you feel in your body? Pleasant, unpleasant, or neutral? Where did you feel it? This is the raw feeling experience before meaning enters.

Perception: How did you interpret the sensation? This is where meaning begins to form. "No response" becomes "something is wrong" or "they don't respect me." Name the interpretation you made.

Mental Formation: What story did you build? This is where interpretation becomes narrative. "They don't respect me" becomes "they never valued my contribution" becomes "I should start looking for another job." Trace the story you constructed.

Consciousness: Can you see the gap between Form and Mental Formation? Remember, the facts themselves are empty. Like the pencil that means something different to the writer, the dog, and the person fighting for their life, "no response for three days" carries no inherent meaning. It is neutral information that could support many different stories. What made you fill the emptiness with the particular meaning you chose? Write out each layer.

Phase Four: Alternative Stories

Because the facts are empty of inherent meaning, they can support multiple interpretations. Creating alternative stories frees up your mind to see there are many possibilities in play and attachment to one narrative isn't working.

Write one to three alternative stories that explain the same facts from Phase Three. Make them as plausible as your original interpretation.

If your original story was "they're ignoring me because they don't value my input," alternatives might be: "they're overwhelmed with something I don't know about," or "my email got buried," or "they're taking time to consider my proposal carefully."

Consider: If someone you trust was observing this same situation, what might they notice that you are missing?

Notice how each alternative story changes what you feel in your body. The facts have not changed. Only the interpretation.

Phase Five: Integration

You have identified the patterns involved and the layers that were stacking up to create a fixed narrative. You have written out alternative stories to free your mind from those fixed viewpoints.

Now, using skillful inquiry: If the situation isn't resolved from the exercise so far, what questions could you ask to get clarity? These questions can be directed to yourself, to someone you trust, or to the person you need clarity with.

Start with these:

- Have I resolved my confusion or judgment about this situation?
- Is it still taxing my mind or getting in the way of my work?
- Is there something I still need to understand from the other person involved?
- What would I need to know from them to move forward clearly?

Choose one question and gather one piece of real-world data within 24 hours.

Adaptations

Quick version: When you notice a strong reaction, ask only: "What are the bare facts?" and "What's one alternative story that fits those facts?" Often this is enough to loosen the grip of certainty.

Deep version: Journal through each layer slowly. Explore the history of this pattern. When did you first learn to see this way? What was it protecting you from? How has it served you, and how has it limited you?

Real-time version: When you catch yourself mid-reaction, pause. Ask: "What pattern is active right now?" and "What am I adding to the facts?" You can run a micro-audit in thirty seconds once the framework is familiar.

Relationship version: After a conflict with someone, do the audit together. Often you will discover you were reacting to different mirages of the same situation.

What to Expect

First few times: You may resist seeing your perception as construction. The story feels true. That is exactly how mirages work. The practice is not about denying your experience but about recognizing that your experience is one interpretation among many possible ones.

After a few times of doing the practice: You will start catching patterns in real-time, noticing "I'm catastrophizing" or "I'm personalizing" as it happens. The gap between stimulus and interpretation widens. You will hold your perceptions more lightly, which helps you see more clearly.

Common Obstacles

"But my interpretation is correct." It might be. The audit is not about proving yourself wrong. It is about testing whether your certainty is warranted, and if there are nuances you may have missed. Most narratives of a situation vary from person to person in some way. If your interpretation holds up after examining the layers and considering alternatives, you have more confidence in it. If it does not, you have saved yourself from acting on a mirage.

"I can do this for small things but not when it really matters." The situations that feel most charged are exactly where this practice matters most. Start with smaller situations to build the skill. Then gradually apply it to higher-stakes perceptions.

Field Note

Opal and I had just started working together. She came to me to help with her public speaking and external client relations. Her role was working with donors for a nonprofit, and she had gotten feedback that she needed to engage with donors in a more meaningful way. It wasn't that her passion or commitment was being questioned, but there was a tendency for her to get lost in her thoughts while speaking with a donor.

When we started off, the first thing that came up was resistance to the idea that this was a valid critique. It was clear that the

Catastrophizer and Polarizer patterns were in play. Opal had built a fixed narrative that she wasn't doing as well as other people in her role. She then inferred that she might not be smart enough to connect with clients in an impactful way.

When she explained to me what her manager was asking for, I didn't hear it that way at all. What I heard was: "We want to invest in you because we believe that you're doing great, and we can coach you into a higher level of performance in the future."

We debunked the Catastrophizer by realizing that the company was investing in her potential. The Polarizer was simply moving between two outcomes: "do this perfectly" or "not at all." We came up with a more nuanced idea of doing her work in a way that was aligned with who she was and optimized her skill sets, which would ultimately yield a unique and valuable addition to the company.

Once we had worked through the patterns, she was able to share the sensation in her body when she was talking to clients. There was a moving tension through her shoulders, neck, and eyes that made it hard to focus. Her mind would get caught up in too many possible answers to a question, and that flustered her. She was interpreting this as not being capable of speaking with clients in complex situations. The narrative she built was that the difficulties she was having were keeping her from being valuable to the company.

Once we started to unpack this, she began to see the emptiness of the situation. The facts could support many interpretations. Instead of learning how to do something better, we could focus on learning how to do something authentically. Once we changed that narrative, the questions became simple: What are situations where you feel like you can connect clearly? How do we work around moments when you're feeling overwhelmed? What's the most valuable thing you bring to every conversation with a donor?

From there, it was easy to align her values with her approach. Her passion for what the nonprofit does. How much she values connecting with people in an authentic way and being present with them. Sharing and reflecting back to donors how much value they bring to the world through their giving.

The shift showed up quickly in her work. She was able to be present in her meetings with donors. She stopped trying to have the right answers and instead reflected back their value and shared her passion. Those simple changes created powerful interactions that changed how donors experienced her and how she experienced herself.

Remember This

The gap between what we experience and what is actually happening can be enormous. We construct false perceptions that feel absolutely true, and unlike the desert traveler who eventually reaches the mirage and finds sand, we often never discover we were seeing illusions at all.

The Five Skandhas reveal how we build our perceived reality layer by layer. We move from raw sensory input through emotional response, interpretation, mental formation, and consciousness. Each layer adds its own potential distortion, until what we take for solid truth is actually an elaborate construction built on top of much simpler facts. The facts themselves are empty of inherent meaning. Like a pencil that means something different to a writer and a dog, every situation we encounter carries no fixed meaning until we fill it with interpretation.

Our perceptual patterns act as invisible filters that determine what information gets through and what remains unseen. The Catastrophizer, the Rationalizer, the Personalizer, the Generalizer, the Polarizer. These are not character flaws but adaptive strategies that become problematic only when they operate outside our awareness. Meanwhile, the digital environments we inhabit amplify these patterns, creating personalized distortion fields that reinforce our biases while making us feel we are seeing objective reality.

Our bodies offer a pathway back to clearer perception. The somatic markers that guide our decisions, the felt sense that something is off, the physical expansion or contraction in response to possibilities all carry wisdom our analytical minds miss. Learning to read these embodied signals while understanding how our patterns shape them helps us navigate between the extremes of pure rationality and unchecked emotion. The invitation here is to develop perceptual literacy: recognizing when we are seeing mirages, understanding how we create them, and consciously choosing to look again.

9

THE OASIS WITHIN

"The end of all our exploring
Will be to arrive where we started
and know the place for the first time."
— T. S. Eliot

In the early 2000s, I was the Chinese Medicine director of an integrated medical center in New York City. In those days, acupuncture, herbal medicine, and meditation were far outside the mainstream as a medical option. We usually saw people who were suffering from severe illnesses, where they had exhausted all other remedies. I loved practicing integrated medicine. I loved the challenge of understanding how I could help someone in a meaningful way, trying to solve the puzzle of their medical issues energetically, physiologically, and psychologically. But until I worked at this cancer clinic, I had never really faced illnesses that were so far along, severe, and often incurable.

The beauty of holistic integrated medicine is that it treats the whole human being through the lens of a natural ecosystem. The metaphor we use for medicine isn't a battlefield or a war between disease and cure, but rather a process of harmonizing and balancing your body and mind.

Patients were not coming to our center for miracle cures. They were coming for support during chemotherapy, pain management, and emotional trauma around the diseases they were dealing with. They came for hope, compassion, and human connection. For someone to walk beside them through one of the hardest things they would do in their lives. It was my calling to help them medically, but to also be their partner, confidant, and friend. People who are very sick tend to get isolated. People are afraid to visit and often don't know what to say to them. It can end up making a brutal experience even worse by feeling lonely. My time in that center with those patients dealing with cancer ended up being a place of unexpected intimacy and connection. When people are dealing with life-threatening illnesses, they don't have time for bullshit. If you're going to talk, you have to be able to go all in with them and talk about the hard things they're facing. I didn't have to be an expert in talk therapy, but I did have to be present, authentic, and honest with them. That experience as a partner and clinician, as a doctor, healer, and friend changed my life forever.

As a medical practitioner, I found that maturity comes in the form of balancing the potential of a treatment while also knowing its limitations. Over the years I got pretty good at this balance. After seeing a few thousand patients, I knew where the limits of my skills were, where the limits of the medicine were, and where the magic could occur. I learned how to be fully present with my patients while also not bringing it home at night.

I managed this through rituals at the end of my day. First came charting notes for my patients, recognizing where they stood, what had helped them, and what had not. I considered whether they should be referred to another specialist or whether we were close to moving the needle and bringing them back into balance. By the time I finished charting, there was a closure to the day that allowed me to leave the medicine at the office and head home clear.

This worked great for me until I started working with a particular patient at the cancer center. We'll call her Jane. She was a young woman in her late twenties with metastatic breast cancer, being treated with radiation and chemotherapy, and using all of our services for support through the treatment. She was using a healthy diet and lifestyle and doing everything that you are supposed to do to create the best possible outcome.

In those days, in the early 2000s, once cancer escaped its initial node and began to spread through the body, it was notoriously difficult to put that demon back in the bottle. It is amazing that medicine has now begun developing targeted cellular therapies that I have seen actually cure metastatic cancers that used to be a ten-month death sentence.

Jane was one of those patients who had the best attitude possible and was not living in denial. She had lived a kind of gifted, beautiful life. She loved her work and her partner. She had an energy about her that was open, kind, and funny. Everyone who met her would fall under her spell. I was her caregiver and care coordinator. We worked very closely together, adjusting her treatments for the symptoms she was experiencing. Her husband always came with her, and the three of us became quite close. In those relationships of practicing medicine with someone dealing with a life-threatening illness, you can't help getting attached. The conversations are about life and death, hopes and fears, they are so intimate that you can't help but feel like you have known each other for ten years after only a few months have passed.

Every few months, Jane's blood work would come in, and we would look for the cell markers that would tell us what the incidence and growth of her cancer was and whether it was down or up. Like most cancer treatments back then, she would get better, and then get worse, and then get better, and then get worse. It was a journey of hope and sometimes joy, and sometimes reprieve, and sometimes sadness. And all the while she would talk about how much she loved living in New York and being in the hustle and bustle of the city, with all of its creativity, inspiration, and potential. She was a designer and loved New York in the way that only happens when people come to the city and actually find the dream they were looking for. Jane was one of those people. Her passion for life, her open, joyful, and loving way of being in the world was contagious and uplifting.

We worked together for about two years, and toward the end of those two years, the cancer had finally overcome her. I continued to do everything I could to support her. Part of that was palliative care and pain management. But the most important aspect of it was just being fully present with her and listening. Often when people are dealing with their life-threatening disease, it is easier to talk to someone in the healer or doctor's role because they feel free to open up about what they are going through instead of having to put on a good front for the family.

There is so much emotional lifting that everyone does when a family faces this kind of situation. It is often a gift to have someone who can listen without needing to be protected. It makes a tremendous difference to be a present witness when you are walking alongside someone going through the journey of dying. Most of the people in the room are terrified or confused about how to talk about what's going on. When people are dying, they have no room for bullshit. They crave authentic presence and need people who can laugh and cry and listen with them. Hospice nurses know this all too well. Those moments of connection, and the creation of a space where everything can be open, honest, and compassionate, are critical ingredients in the recipe for dying well. "It's not going to be ok." I'd say, and she'd take a deep breath in, exhale and we would laugh, relieved by getting to take off the "put on a cheerful face" expectation everyone had when they came to see her.

Two days before Jane died, her husband called me and asked me to come over to the house to say goodbye to her. "Of course," I said, without thinking. I had been with my mother when she died, and my father. But they were older, and somehow it made sense. I had been with other patients close to when they had passed, but to see this woman who was younger than me, who had been so alive and filled with excitement about being alive, suddenly be facing the end of her life was an injustice I was not prepared for. Her body had wasted away. Her mind was still present but struggling to parse this world from the next. I just could not manage how cruel the universe seemed at that moment.

I sat beside her in her room, held her hand, and said goodbye. I thanked her for all the time that we had spent together and promised I would be there for her husband. After a time, she slipped into sleep, and I gave her husband a long hug and silently made my way out of their five-story Brooklyn walk-up. I managed to somehow remain stable and composed through that entire experience, but the moment that I walked outside of the front door of their brownstone and onto the street, I just burst into tears. Heaving and sobbing on the street outside the bodega on the corner.

Walking Into the Desert

The thing about the desert is that you walk into its beauty, not realizing its vastness. You go for a walk into the sand because it grabs your attention, and you think, "Let's see what's out there. It looks so amazing." The problem with this point of view is that it is an abstraction. The beauty of the desert from a distance, with its creamy wave-like hills and windswept valleys, is mesmerizing. However, the reality of the desert is that if you are not prepared with hydration, sun protection, and an understanding of how its ecosystem operates, in no time, you are so far out of your depth that you find yourself asking, "How did I get here, and how will I ever get back?"

The moment I left Jane's apartment that day, I realized I had walked into the desert unprepared and prayed I could survive while I found my way back.

We see the vision of where we are trying to go in our lives, and somewhere along the way—usually after we have gone far enough into the unknown, we realize what we have gotten ourselves into and that we do not have all the tools to find our way home.

In the desert, you slowly start to notice the incredible dryness of the air and that the sun is brighter and burning hotter than you ever thought it could. You begin to sense the magnitude of the event that you have placed yourself in. There is a shift that happens once the shock of the realization subsides.

It comes in the form of an invitation to stillness. A moment of acceptance of the situation for what it is. Once you arrive at acceptance, you can begin to grow and adapt. Stillness and observation are the keystones. As you survey the desert over time, you start to notice how it stays hidden and quiet during the day and comes to life at night. How careful the desert creatures are with their energy, and how unforgiving it can be when a mistake is made. For me, it took some time to grieve Jane's loss before I could begin to find my way back from that desert. Stillness is an integral part of so many rituals around death for just this reason. We need time to make our way back from devastating loss, time to integrate into the new orientation of someone being gone forever. Of whom we are without them.

There are times in your life where you will find yourself in a desert moment. It will be a place where you are out of your depth, and the resources that you brought in are not the ones that will get you through. In those moments, if you adapt and learn new skills, you can come out of it wiser, stronger, clearer, and more open-hearted. Desert moments are our most difficult and are often followed by some of the most rewarding times. They will serve us throughout the rest of our lives and offer a depth of purpose, perspective, and compassion that can only be earned through those kinds of experiences.

At the end of Jane's life, I found myself in the overwhelming confusion of that desert moment. I was completely unprepared for the raw emotion and bizarre detachment it evoked in me. I wasn't prepared for the pain that came with not being able to save her or her husband from that pain. And that was just the beginning.

The confluence of stressors in my life at that time was a perfect storm. Our cancer center was also struggling to survive. New York had been devastated by the Twin Tower attacks, leaving the city and country in a state of raw uncertainty that we had never known before. I had come to care so deeply for a patient that I had stopped walking beside her and gotten lost in the momentum of her life ending. All these forces together left me lost in despair and confusion. I thought, "What's my path forward?" How do I navigate through this desert? I was emotionally and physically exhausted. I was desperate for a way out of the whole experience, but that is the thing about the desert. You are too far in when you realize where you are, to turn back. The only way out is through. I knew I had to adapt, but I did not know how. I felt paralyzed, unsure of the path forward.

When I was a kid, my father would say: "If you don't make a decision, the world makes one for you." It turned out this was going to be one of those moments where dad's fatherly wisdom would come true. A week later, I found out the cancer center was closing in ten days. I had to tie up any loose ends with my patients and find new places for them to go. I also had no choice but to figure out what I was going to do next. I had known the company was in trouble, but I did not realize how bad. We had all been kept in the dark about the severity of the situation. It turned out the founders were hoping for a miracle that never came through. The decision of what to do next was made for me by the company. I knew I would continue to practice medicine, but for the moment, it was time to let this part of my life come to an end.

In the *I Ching*, the *Daoist Book of Changes*, it says: "Before action, there is stillness." This was what was next for me. I had to find a place of stillness and center myself. To recognize the ecosystem, I was in and understand how to balance my life within it.

I knew I had to let go and grieve all the different losses I was experiencing, from Jane's death to the fall of this innovative medical clinic, to the new vulnerability of terrorist attacks in our city. I felt like I had failed in so many ways. My career was upside down. I had lost a friend and patient and had no idea what to do with those feelings. I was having survivor's guilt on so many different fronts. Why her and not me? Why the Twin Towers and not where I was ten blocks away? What gives me the right to go forward while others who fought so passionately for their lives are denied?

The Seed of New Life

In the weeks after, as I took time to let myself feel into the pain of these losses, I started to notice an understanding come through. It is so cliché that I hate to even put it into words here, but in my early life with its uncertainty, chaos, and danger, I had never really thought that I would live all that long. So I had a cavalier attitude. I was willing to take risks that others would not take. Through no skill of my own, it served me well. Others would tell me how courageous I was, and although I liked the idea of that, deep down, I knew they were wrong. What everyone else had thought was fearlessness I would come to realize was ignorance.

After going through this experience, I realized that I had never truly appreciated my life. I had thought of life as a battlefield with no chance of winning. I used this point of view as a way to have no expectations and deny the hope of a long and meaningful life. I had always known the wonder of the sunrise and the sweetness of its warmth on my skin, but it was a fleeting quality for me, of a world that was always slipping away. A world I was sure I did not really belong to.

After a few weeks of grieving, I started to feel the green shoots of a new life emerging in me. My perception began shifting. I didn't realize at first what was happening, but as I healed from these losses, and especially from Jane's death, there was a new seed of appreciation for life growing in me. She had given me one last lesson. Inside this seed was the incredible joy and gratitude for the gift that is my life. To hug someone and feel the exchange of our energy through our bodies, to savor a delicious meal as though it were my last, to see an old friend again, to share in the stories of our past. All of this had gone from black and white and distant, to brilliant technicolor and present in my heart.

This experience is at the heart of what we call mindfulness. It is not paying close attention to the moment. It is being completely present with all of your senses and spirit in the moment.

I knew at a deeper, more permanent level that this was the moment when I was given the opportunity to step completely onto my path. It was the first time in my life that as I imagined my way forward, it was filled with the joy of creation and connection.

That was my Oasis moment. Like seeing water in the middle of the desert, with trees giving shade all around it. I found myself alive again with the force and energy of a new beginning. Like the creativity that only comes from a blank slate, I started to feel deep in my bones the unfolding of the journey.

Your desert moment offers you a blank slate, the freedom that comes from not knowing what's next, but knowing you are going to have the resources to step into it. So, as you navigate the tempest of the desert, remember to try and keep an open heart and an eye on the horizon for your Oasis moment. This place is the realization that renewal and recovery often happen in the most unexpected places. Although my example is a massive pivot in my life, the oasis can be a moment on a difficult day when a friend reaches out for a coffee. The oasis is always available to us. Our capacity for recovery, renewal, and growth emerges from these Oasis moments, transforming how we engage with challenges and discover new possibilities for magic in our everyday lives.

The Modern Desert

The modern world often feels like an endless queue of demands and expectations. We move from task to task, meeting to meeting, constantly connected by our technology yet increasingly disconnected from the sources of renewal. Since the industrial revolution, the metrics of success have become tied to output and productivity, leaving little room for the essential practice of replenishment, and the joy of just being.

In a world where growth constantly needs to increase to satisfy the stakeholders of business, practices of sustainability, of knowing how to use the oasis to recover and find the natural rhythm of effort and nourishment, are often overlooked. Our expectations for output seem to keep increasing in an attempt to keep up with the speed of our technology. In the book *Nexus* by Yuval Noah Harari, he references the idea that One of the biggest threats to humanity from artificial intelligence is our need to rest. As AI is always on, humans have no opportunity to escape the relentless pace of the machine world.

Recent studies suggest that over 70 percent of professionals report feeling depleted at least once per week, with many experiencing this state daily. We have created a culture that celebrates the endless sprint but has forgotten the importance of rest, recovery, and celebration. Life is cyclic in nature. It rises and falls, just like our cortisol levels do every day. These neurotransmitters and hormones kick in with the rising sun, waking us up in the morning, and fall with the setting sun, letting our bodies quiet down and recover.

Finding the Oasis in Professional Life

I witnessed this pattern clearly while working with Alex, a tech startup product director whose company was on a tight timeline to build a new AI product for a very large client. This client was an anchor investor as well as one of the first major enterprise clients for the company, so the pressure to deliver a flawless product was extremely high.

At first glance, Alex appeared to be in his element, driving results, working through difficulties. But after a couple of sessions together, the veneer began to show its cracks. "I feel like I'm running on fumes," he admitted. "I can't get the team to deliver at the speed that I need them to. Even when they agree on deliverables and deadlines, we still somehow aren't there when we get to the finish line."

He was frustrated and stuck in a loop, trying to solve the problem with the same approach over and over. My definition of frustration is the distance between how you wish things were and how things actually are. To close that gap, we have to see the situation through a more neutral lens.

The pivotal moment for Alex came when he realized that he needed to address his own exhaustion before he could effectively guide his team. He was depleted and had lost his ability to nourish himself, and with that had lost the ability to investigate and adapt. His old strategy of powering through was not working anymore. He was overwhelmed by the pressure of deadlines. What he needed was perspective, an oasis to revitalize his system and allow his mind to relax and open enough to see the complexity of the problem in front of him.

We created "Oasis Moments" in his week. Dedicated time where he would focus on zooming out and seeing the whole system he was working in. Taking a moment to step into the conductor's role and tune the orchestra to see how all the musicians were connecting and communicating with each other.

This practice gave him the mental space and actual time to shift his perception, to be in stillness long enough to discover a new solution. When he did this, his path forward became clear. He identified where the teams were miscommunicating, and by tweaking their process, he was able to create a new process for building. He created an oasis for himself that translated into one for the whole team.

The Three Levels

Alex's situation reflected a common problem. Those who most need renewal often do not realize it and stay in a depletion loop. When I meet clients who find themselves in a space like Alex's, we use the Oasis Practice. It is a practical approach to identifying and cultivating sources of restoration and vitality. Cultivating in this sense is the same as caring for a garden. The output of your garden can easily increase over time with care, even though the size of the garden stays the same. Mindful, balanced cultivation can create rich output. When you understand an entire ecosystem, you can harmonize with its needs and resources to sustainably increase its output.

Think of a professional athlete. When we watch them perform, we see just the visible result of their commitment. Behind the scenes, they are constantly optimizing through practices like strength training, careful nutrition, coaching sessions, meditation, quality sleep, and physical therapy. They are always taking steps to improve their chances of success. It is no different for you. But here is the key distinction: your performance is not limited to just your job. It encompasses your entire life. So, ask yourself: How are you optimizing for the work achievements you desire? Are you finding joy, creativity, and satisfaction in your life? Are you strengthening your connections with friends, family, and colleagues? Are you taking time to reflect on your journey and identify the growth path most aligned with who you are? All these elements are essential pieces of living, and they are all better when we are following a natural aligned rhythm.

Pick a way of viewing your life, like the athlete, a gardener, or any system that resonates with you. Then use that viewpoint as your operating model. All the different things you do, whether it is physical training, a work sprint, or taking time to watch clouds in the sky, all of it matters. It is all woven into the fabric of your daily existence and creates a flexible system that you can adjust every day. This framing is how you infuse mindfulness into your days; the practice brings conscious intent into your days. You create your own Dao or Way of your life.

The Oasis Practice operates on three levels: Recognition, Resonance, and Integration.

Recognition involves developing awareness of your personal depletion signals. These vary for each person but often include physical indicators like disrupted sleep or physical tension, emotional markers such as increased irritability or decreased creativity, and mental signs like difficulty focusing or decision fatigue. Alex's signals included chronic lower back pain, insomnia, and an inability to engage in strategic thinking, his usual strength.

Resonance explores what activities, environments, or practices naturally restore you. This is not about prescribing universal solutions but discovering what uniquely recharges you personally. For some, renewal comes through intensive rock-climbing sessions. For others, it emerges through stillness, daily journaling, or stepping into water. Find yours.

Integration focuses on weaving these renewal points into the fabric of daily life. This is perhaps the most crucial and challenging aspect. It is not enough to identify what replenishes you. You must create sustainable ways to access these sources regularly.

For Alex, the breakthrough came when he recognized that control was both his greatest strength and his most limiting vulnerability. Through our work together, we mapped out how he defined control and where he sought it in his work. We discovered an important distinction: while his need for control genuinely helped him stay organized and maintain visibility on team progress and product goals, his attempts to force productivity levels beyond the team's capacity created an illusion of control that ultimately led to failure.

Once we identified this pattern, we could work with it constructively. We anchored the aspects of control that served him well: his organizational systems, his tracking methods, his clear communication of goals. Then, in the areas where rigid control was failing him, we introduced a different approach: controlled exploration through clarifying questions. This combination gave him the stability he needed while creating space for discovery. Rather than forcing outcomes, he learned to guide his team through inquiry, uncovering new ways of working together that he could never have mandated into existence.

Practice: The Oasis Map

Applied Insights

The capacity to recognize depletion patterns and locate sources of renewal that actually restore you. This practice trains you to map your personal desert terrain, discover hidden springs where depletion itself reveals unexpected gifts, and cultivate oases at different scales. Over time, you develop sustainable rhythms of effort and restoration.

When to Use

- When you feel depleted but cannot identify why
- When rest is not restoring you
- When you are entering a demanding period and want to plan for sustainability
- When you notice one element consistently undermining the others
- When your usual recovery strategies have stopped working
- As a periodic audit to maintain your renewal systems

The Practice

Find 20 minutes of quiet space with paper or a journal. This practice is not about solving a specific problem. It's about mapping where you're depleted and discovering what restores you.

You'll survey three types of depletion, look for hidden wisdom in what your exhaustion might be teaching you, and identify renewal practices at different scales. The goal is to build a sustainable rhythm of effort and restoration.

Phase One: Desert Survey

Create three columns on a page in your journal:

- Physical Depletion
- Mental/Emotional Depletion
- Purpose Depletion

Under Physical Depletion, note where and when your body is depleted. Is this the satisfying fatigue from meaningful effort or hollow exhaustion from misaligned action? Where does it show up first in your body? Shoulders, gut, sleep quality, appetite?

Under Mental/Emotional Depletion, identify draining thought patterns and emotional states. What beliefs underlie this depletion? What are you trying to control that is beyond your control? What emotions have been dominant?

Under Purpose Depletion, explore where you feel disconnected from meaning. What activities feel empty of significance? What once inspired you but now feels hollow? Where are you going through the motions?

Rate each column from one to ten, where one is severely depleted, and ten is fully resourced.

Phase Two: Hidden Springs

This phase reverses the usual approach. Instead of fighting depletion, look for the wisdom it might be revealing.

For each depletion area, ask: If this depletion is trying to teach me something, what is it?

If exhaustion forces you to slow down, what becomes visible in that stillness? If mental depletion breaks your usual approach, what new thinking might emerge? If purpose depletion is draining your motivation, what is it pointing you away from or toward?

Write one or two examples from your life when depletion led to an unexpected renewal of something. Maybe illness forced rest that led to realization. Perhaps failure opened doors to more innovative solutions. A period of emptiness may have preceded your most significant growth.

Depletion is not always the enemy. Sometimes it is a guide.

Phase Three: Rhythm Recognition

Map your depletion and renewal patterns across different time scales.

Daily Rhythms: When does your energy naturally rise and fall? When are you most vital? When does depletion typically occur? How do you currently work with or against these rhythms?

Weekly Patterns: Which days or activities create cumulative depletion? Which creates restoration? Is there a pattern to when you crash or when you feel most resourced?

Seasonal Cycles: Recognize longer patterns in project cycles, work rhythms, or life phases. When does depletion serve a purpose, preparing ground for renewal? When is it simply unsustainable?

Write what you notice about your rhythms at each scale.

Phase Four: Oasis Cultivation

Create practices at three different scales that honor both your depletion patterns and your need for renewal.

Micro-Oases: Brief practices you can access even when depleted. Take a few minutes of slow breathing. A focused and specific moment of gratitude. Stepping outside for fresh air, taking a walking meeting. Acknowledging depletion without resistance. List two to three micro-oases that work for you.

Structural Oases: Schedule or environment changes that create regular renewal. Protected transition time between meetings. A weekly practice that restores you. Environmental modifications that reduce unnecessary depletion. Boundaries like focus time, that prevent energy leaks. List one to three structural oases you can implement.

Deep Oases: Periodic deep renewal that allows full restoration. Quarterly retreats. Seasonal practices. Extended time in nature. Recognizing when life forces renewal through unexpected events and accepting rather than fighting it. List one to two depth oases that serve you. My favorite is the dopamine detox.

Phase Five: Integration

Identify one insight about the relationship between your depletion and renewal. What did this mapping reveal that you had not seen clearly?

Choose one practice from each oasis category to implement right away:

- One micro-oasis to use daily
- One structural oasis to put in place
- One depth oasis to schedule

Start small. Practices you can maintain even when depleted matter more than ambitious plans that collapse under pressure.

Set up a specific result like sleep, or mood stability, etc. Pay attention to the results. They will show the impact of your actions. If they aren't aligned with your expectations, pause and reassess.

Adaptations

Quick version (10 minutes): Skip to Phase Four. Identify one micro-oasis, one structural oasis, and one depth oasis. Implement the micro-oasis today.

Deep version (60+ minutes): Expand Phase Two into a full exploration of your history with depletion and renewal. Journal about times when breakdown became breakthrough. Explore what your current depletion might be preparing you for.

Weekly check-in version: Create a simple tracking practice. Note which depletions felt meaningful versus hollow; which renewals restored versus merely distracted. This builds your ability to distinguish between different qualities of both states.

Crisis version: When severely depleted, skip the mapping. Go directly to your micro-oasis list and do one now. Even small renewal interrupts the depletion spiral.

What to Expect

First few times: You may struggle to see depletion as anything other than a problem to fix. The Hidden Springs phase may feel counterintuitive. You may also discover how disconnected you have become from your natural rhythms and what actually restores you versus what you do out of habit.

After a few times of doing the practice: You will develop fluency with your personal depletion signals, catching them earlier. The three scales of oases become a reliable framework. You will start treating renewal as essential maintenance rather than occasional rescue.

Common Obstacles

"I don't have time for renewal." This is often the voice of depletion itself. Start with micro-oases. You can always find ninety seconds in your day. Something small and real beats something ideal and imaginary. As micro-oases prove their value, structural oases become easier to protect.

"Nothing seems to restore me anymore." When standard oases stop working, look at the Purpose column from Phase One. The depletion may be signaling misalignment that rest alone cannot address. Return to Phase Two and ask what this depletion might be trying to teach you.

Field Note

Colin had been running hard for two years. Building a startup, merging it with another company, and designing a new product. For the final nine months, he was working fourteen-hour days. When he finally stepped away, his body was depleted and his mind could not stop reaching for the next problem to solve.

We made an agreement. Six weeks with no work, no planning for the future, no trying to figure out what came next. His only job was to stop.

He decided to travel. The details matter less than what he practiced while traveling: dismantling the habit of productivity. Every time his mind lunged toward planning or strategizing, he let it go. Every time the drive to build something arose, he watched it without acting. He was learning to rest in "being without doing".

When I saw him after those six weeks, I almost did not recognize him. The tension had drained from his face. His eyes were clear and bright. He sat down, and his body actually settled into the chair, no longer coiled for the next sprint.

"I don't have a plan," he said. "I didn't figure out my next move." He paused. "But I found this place in myself. This deep, open, and quiet. And I know that whatever I do next needs to be about creating something that matters to me. Not just building to build.

A week later, he called me. A friend had mentioned an idea he had been sitting on for months: a company designed to help people support each other's growth in small, committed groups. The friend had the vision but had not been able to move it forward.

Colin, in his restored state, saw immediately what his friend could not see. Within three days, he had built out the website, the product structure, and a roadmap for the first year. He sent it to his friend, who was stunned.

That company is now in its second year and growing fast.

Remember This

Renewal is not a luxury but an essential component of sustainable performance and growth. We have created a culture that celebrates the endless sprint but forgotten the importance of rest, recovery, and celebration. Life is cyclic in nature. It rises and falls just like our cortisol levels do every day.

The desert moments in our lives, those times when we find ourselves outside our depth with resources that will not get us through, are often our most difficult and most rewarding experiences. They serve us throughout the rest of our lives and offer a depth of purpose, perspective, and understanding that can only be earned through experience. The only way out is through.

The Oasis Practice operates on three levels. Recognition develops awareness of your personal depletion signals. Resonance explores what activities, environments, or practices naturally restore you. Integration focuses on weaving these renewal points into the fabric of daily life. It is not enough to identify what replenishes you. You must create sustainable ways to access these sources regularly.

Think of the desert itself, a seemingly harsh environment that nevertheless supports remarkable life through hidden systems of renewal and resilience. The desert teaches us that sustainability is not about constant abundance but about knowing how to find and preserve the sources of vitality available to us. As you navigate your own personal and professional deserts, the practice of finding and creating oases becomes not just a survival skill but your path to thriving.

10

RECLAIMING YOUR SHADOW

"One does not become enlightened by imagining figures of light, but by making the darkness conscious."
— Carl Jung

Three years ago, I stood at a crossroads that would fundamentally change my life and work. After decades of building a successful Chinese medicine practice in New York City, a practice where I had helped thousands of patients and established deep roots in the community, I was preparing to walk away from it all. The opportunity before me was both exhilarating and terrifying: to relocate my family across the country to Boulder, Colorado, to embed myself at TIFIN, a fintech startup, as their Chief Mindfulness Officer.

This wasn't just a career change. It was a grand experiment to test whether the contemplative technologies of Daoism, self-discovery, and embodied practices could become the foundation for a culture of conscious leadership in the business world. For years, I had taught and written about transformation, about how ancient wisdom could reshape modern leadership. But I had never tested the theory from inside a company. I had proven their value in my one-on-one coaching, but I didn't know if it could scale and foster a meaningful shift under the intense pressure of a fast-moving startup.

One night while thinking about this question, I found myself walking in the woods, my mind racing with possibilities and doubts. I had brought a flashlight to navigate in the dark. As I switched it on, the beam cut sharply through the night, illuminating the path directly ahead with perfect clarity. I noticed that the areas just beyond my light seemed darker than ever, as if the brightness of my beam had deepened the surrounding shadows.

On impulse, I switched off the flashlight. At first, I couldn't see anything. A little twinge of anxiety went through my body. After all, there were bears and mountain lions in our woods. With the light off, I felt their world all around me. But as my eyes slowly adjusted to the darkness, the forest transformed. In the moonlight, I could see the path before me, and the entire landscape of trees and moss, rocks, and logs along the ground. The whole scene was sketched in soft silver light. Without the flashlight's beam, I could perceive the wholeness of where I stood.

This moment became my metaphor for the difficulty I was having with my decision to leave. My medical practice was my flashlight, a focused beam that illuminated a specific path with clarity and precision. It was familiar, effective, and safe. I knew how to walk it and pretty much what it would look like. But there was something calling me to turn off that flashlight, to venture into the uncertainty of the darkness, trusting that my eyes would adjust and reveal a larger landscape of possibility and discovery.

Later, I would realize that I was experiencing what Brené Brown describes as the essential nature of vulnerability in leadership. The shadow I faced scared the hell out of me: What if I couldn't translate my work into the business world? What if the concepts that seemed so powerful in my practice proved ineffective in a startup environment? What if I was full of crap and just didn't know it? Plus, the financial risk was real. If it didn't work, I had no network in Colorado, and my family was financially dependent on me. It felt reckless, but deep down, I knew I had to do it. Real growth often feels reckless. Listen carefully. If there is a voice inside you that knows you must take a leap and find out what's on the other side, then you just have to listen to it. Besides, Jane had already taught me that we only regret the things we didn't do. Leadership is often about stepping into the unknown and forging a path for others to walk.

This journey into the shadows of my own doubts taught me that sometimes the most piercing clarity emerges not from the bright light of certainty, but from walking in the moonlit landscape of vulnerability and risk, fueled by courage and curiosity.

The Dual Nature of Seeing

This idea of different kinds of seeing, flashlight versus moonlight, is central to understanding how we navigate both our inner and outer landscapes. In my years of practicing Chinese medicine alongside Western medical specialists, I witnessed firsthand how these two approaches represented fundamentally different ways of perceiving disease and healing.

Western medicine excels at isolating specific problems through focused diagnostic technologies, like shining a powerful flashlight on a particular organ or system. This approach has given us remarkable capabilities to identify and address specific conditions with precision and clarity. When you need heart surgery or have broken a bone, the focused beam of Western medicine illuminates exactly what needs attention.

Chinese medicine, by contrast, operates more like moonlight perception. It sees the body as an integrated energy system where patterns of disharmony manifest across multiple symptoms and systems. A Chinese medicine practitioner might look at ten seemingly unrelated symptoms and recognize them as a unified pattern that wouldn't be visible under the focused beam of specialized Western diagnosis.

Neither approach is inherently superior. Each reveals different aspects of health. The flashlight's brilliance shows us details with unmatched clarity, while moonlight perception reveals patterns and relationships that remain invisible to focused attention. Together, they offer complementary ways of understanding complex situations.

This dual nature of perception extends far beyond medicine. In leadership, in relationships, and in our inner work, we constantly navigate between these two modes of seeing. The focused beam of analytical thinking helps us solve specific problems, while the moonlit awareness of intuitive perception helps us sense emerging patterns and possibilities.

But here's the challenge: our modern world overwhelmingly values and rewards flashlight perception. We celebrate specialization, detailed analysis, and confident certainty. We often lack the capacity to perceive and value what lies in the shadows beyond that beam. Our fears, intuitive knowledge, emotional undercurrents, and patterns that can only be seen when we allow ourselves to soften and open into our shadows. Some of our greatest insights and growth come from the places we don't want to go.

The Shadow's Wisdom

What exactly do we mean by "the shadow," and why does it matter for our growth and leadership? The concept was first formalized by Carl Jung, who used it to describe those aspects of ourselves that we've disowned, repressed, or pushed into unconsciousness. These aren't necessarily negative qualities. They can include any aspects of ourselves that didn't receive approval or felt unsafe to express.

Shadow material typically falls into several categories. There are the parts of ourselves we've learned to hide because they weren't acceptable in our families or cultures, perhaps our anger, vulnerability, or ambition. There are the qualities we've disowned because they contradict our conscious self-image. The competent professional might repress their uncertainty, the caring parent might deny their resentment, the strong leader might hide their fear.

What makes shadow work so powerful is that these disowned aspects don't simply disappear. They operate beneath the surface, influencing our decisions, relationships, and effectiveness in ways we don't recognize. As Brené Brown's research demonstrates, "What we don't own, owns us." The defensive postures we adopt, the strong reactions we have to certain people or situations; these are often signals of unexamined shadow material seeking integration.

But here's the truth that makes shadow work so transformative: our shadows contain not only our wounds but also some of our greatest gifts. The leader who has disowned their vulnerability may find that reconnecting with it unlocks a new level of authentic connection with their team. The perfectionist who has rejected their limitations may discover that embracing imperfection leads to greater creativity and innovation.

The Three Shadows of Leadership

Through working with leaders across diverse organizations, I've observed that shadow material typically manifests in three distinct but interrelated forms. Understanding these "three shadows of leadership" provides a practical framework to explore your shadows.

The Shadow of Strengths

Our greatest capabilities often cast the darkest shadows. The analytical leader's precision may blind them to intuitive insights. The visionary's imagination may obscure practical limitations. The decisive executive's bias for action may cause them to miss subtle relational dynamics.

The strength itself isn't the problem. It's the shadow it casts when overused or treated as the only valid approach. I experienced this directly at TIFIN when my strength in creating contemplative experiences initially blinded me to the company's legitimate need for measurable outcomes. What had been a gift in my coaching practice became a limitation in the corporate context until I could recognize and integrate this shadow.

Right now, before reading further, name your single greatest strength as a leader. The capability you lean on most. Got it?

Now here's the uncomfortable question: Who on your team or in your life consistently sees things you miss? Chances are, they're seeing from the exact angle your strength creates a blind spot. The analytical leader misses emotional dynamics. The visionary leader overlooks operational details. The decisive leader doesn't notice when people need more time to process.

Your strength isn't the problem. The problem is assuming your strength shows you everything. Notice today when someone brings you information that feels uncomfortable, that's where you'll find your shadow.

The Shadow of Wounds

As the Daoists are fond of saying: "As above so below." Our unhealed experiences create filters that shape who we are in ways we don't recognize. The leader who experienced early betrayal becomes hypervigilant about loyalty. The executive passed over for promotion fixates on recognition. The entrepreneur who grew up with scarcity hoards resources even when abundance is available.

I learned the power of collective wounds (group-reinforced perception) through personal loss. Throughout his life, my brother inhabited a narrative of struggle, a fixed story where he stood alone against an unforgiving world. This wasn't just his perception. It was one we built together as a family, each of us contributing our own part of the wound to the narrative.

I was afraid of my brother and didn't trust him because he was dangerous to me as a child. My father rejected him for being too much of a mirror, carrying alcoholism and addiction into the next generation. My mother felt guilty for not protecting him and for not being able to steer him back on course. My middle sisters feared him. My oldest sister felt a kindred spirit with him but also a sense that she couldn't reach him. Together, we created a view of him as someone who would not be able to recover, and so, at some point along the way, we stopped trying and let him go.

That collective view made it impossible for us to see the moments that emerged where he might have been able to change his trajectory. After his death at fifty-two years old, I could see those moments in retrospect. Times when something shifted in him, when a different path became briefly visible. But our shared perception, reinforced by each person's individual wound, kept us from recognizing those openings. We confused our habitual way of seeing him with the complete truth of who he was and what was possible for him. I don't blame us for this. But I also see the limitations in our perception. If I faced that situation now, I would like to think I would be able to offer a different way of seeing him to the family, and maybe a different path for him to walk.

Think about your own family system or your current team. What fixed story have you all agreed on about someone? "Sarah's difficult." "Tom never follows through."

Now ask: What evidence contradicts that story that everyone's ignoring? What small shifts in that person's behavior go unnoticed because they don't fit the narrative? What shadow am I avoiding in myself by labeling them? Fixed stories about others often reveal our own unhealed wounds projected outward.

The Shadow of Values

What we most strongly reject often points to disowned aspects of ourselves that contain important wisdom. This is what Jung called the "golden shadow," positive qualities we've pushed away because they didn't fit our self-concept or were threatening to our identity.

The leader who dismisses "soft skills" may be protecting themselves from their own need for emotional connection. The executive who judges others for "playing politics" might be denying their own desire for influence. The entrepreneur who scorns "work-life balance" is avoiding their own need for rest and renewal.

I confronted this shadow in the business world when I initially judged the company's focus on metrics as somehow less meaningful than subjective transformation. This judgment protected me from facing my fear that my work might not produce measurable results. By integrating my shadow around measurement, I developed approaches that honor both depth and demonstrable impact.

What quality do you judge most harshly in others? Write it down. Be specific. "People who need constant validation." "Leaders who can't make decisions." "Those who prioritize feelings over facts."

Now sit with this uncomfortable possibility: that quality you judge might be something you need more of in your own life. The person who judges "needy" people might need to look at how comfortable they are with asking for help. The one who scorns indecision might need to slow down and gather more perspectives. Your harshest judgments are often the doorway to your highest self. But you have to walk through it.

The Paradox of Illumination

One of the most fascinating aspects of shadow work is what I call the Paradox of Illumination: the brightest light often creates the darkest shadows. Areas where we have the greatest clarity, confidence, and capability generate our most significant blind spots precisely because we never think to question them.

This paradox manifests in predictable patterns. Deep expertise in a domain often creates what researchers call "functional fixedness," where masters become so attached to established patterns, they can't see simpler solutions. Success narratives conceal future failure because we selectively remember our successes while forgetting or reframing our failures.

The deeper insight: Our greatest strengths, when unbalanced by shadow awareness, become our greatest liabilities. The confidence that enables decisive leadership becomes dangerous without the humility of recognizing what we don't see.

Working with Shadows

Given these challenges of perceiving our own shadows, how do we develop the ability to see beyond the beam of our conscious focus into the rich landscape of the unconscious?

Shadow work begins with creating conditions for shadow material to emerge safely. Just as our eyes need time to adjust to darkness, our awareness needs space to perceive what lies beyond habitual attention. Three approaches prove particularly effective:

Creating Space for the Unconscious: Our shadows communicate through channels our everyday awareness overlooks: dreams, body sensations, creative expression, and unexpected emotions. The practices from earlier chapters become essential here. Dream journaling captures the unconscious mind's symbolic communications. Body scan meditations cultivate awareness of somatic signals. Movement practices bypass cognitive control. Time in nature shifts us from analytical to receptive awareness.

Recognizing Projections: What triggers us in others often signals our own shadow material. We react most strongly to qualities that resonate with disowned aspects of ourselves. The intensity of our reaction correlates with the importance of shadow material. When you find yourself having a disproportionate reaction to someone, ask what part of yourself you're seeing in them.

Developing Comfort with Paradox: Shadow integration requires holding opposing truths simultaneously. We can be both strong and vulnerable, both certain and curious, both teacher and student. As Bill George, author of *Authentic Leadership* notes, authentic leaders acknowledge their shadows while leading from their strengths.

Practice: Shadow Integration

Applied Insights

The capacity to recognize and integrate the parts of yourself you've disowned, repressed, or pushed into unconsciousness. This practice trains you to read your strong reactions as signals of shadow material, discover what those shadows are protecting, and bring them into conscious relationship with your whole self. Over time, you reclaim energy that was spent on suppression and access gifts that were hidden in the darkness.

When to Use

- When you have a disproportionately strong reaction to someone or something
- When you notice yourself judging others harshly for a specific quality
- When the same issue shows up across different situations
- When you sense a blind spot but can't see it directly
- When a strength has become a limitation
- As ongoing practice for continued self-discovery

The Practice

Most importantly, embracing our shadows is how we grow. Integration allows us to work with these difficulties rather than fight them. If you find yourself resisting this practice, remember that accepting your darkness is how you step into the light.

You'll work with your strong reactions as doorways. Consider recent moments where your response felt disproportionate to the situation. Emotions like anger, defensiveness, judgment, sadness, or shame that surprised you with its intensity. These are signals pointing to your shadow material.

Phase One: Trigger Mapping

Bring to mind a situation where you experienced an unexpectedly strong emotional response. These might be moments of anger, defensiveness, judgment, envy, desire, or shame. The strength of your reaction is the signal, not the cause.

Write what specifically triggered you. Look for the quality or behavior that activated you rather than the circumstances. Here are some examples: Was it someone questioning your competence? Maybe someone who was achieving at a level beyond you, and where you thought you should be. A person avoiding an obvious truth? Someone needing too much validation?

Now look for patterns across your examples. Most people discover they have two or three core triggers that show up in different forms across situations. Common patterns cluster around:

- *Authority:* Being questioned, challenged, or overruled
- *Competence:* Mistakes, uncertainty, being seen as inadequate
- *Belonging:* Exclusion, difference, not fitting in
- *Value:* Feeling valued for what they bring to the table every day

Write down the trigger pattern you identified.

Phase Two: The Three Shadows Check

Your trigger likely connects to one of three shadow types. Identify which one resonates most:

Shadow of Strengths: Your greatest capabilities cast the darkest shadows. The analytical leader's precision blinds them to intuitive insights. The visionary's imagination obscures practical limitations. What is your greatest strength, and what might it be preventing you from seeing?

Shadow of Wounds: Unhealed experiences create perceptual filters. The leader who experienced early betrayal becomes hypervigilant about loyalty, often missing key growth because of it. The person passed over for promotion fixates on recognition. The person betrayed by a loved one struggles with trusting their partner. What old wound might be shaping how you see this trigger?

Shadow of Values: What we reject in others often points to disowned parts of ourselves. The leader who dismisses "soft skills" may be protecting themselves from their own need for connection. What quality do you judge most harshly in others, and how might you need more of it yourself?

Name which shadow type feels most active with your primary trigger, and why. Link the shadow and trigger to an early cause if you can.

Phase Three: Mirror Work

This is the difficult part. Ask yourself: How does this quality I'm reacting to exist in me, even if it looks different?

If you judge people for needing validation, where do you seek approval in ways you don't acknowledge? If you react strongly to indecisiveness, where does your own certainty cover uncertainty? If someone's emotional expression triggers you, where do you suppress your own feelings?

Write what you discover. This isn't about self-blame. It's about growth through recognition.

Ask: What is this shadow trying to protect me from? The shadow usually has a positive intention beneath its manifestation. It developed for a reason. What need was it serving? What would you lose if you let it go? What might you gain?

Phase Four: Dialogue

Create space for an internal dialogue between your conscious self and this shadow aspect. This is a form of visualization that helps you make a genuine inquiry into a part of yourself that's only been speaking through reactions rather than language. Remember, language is how we encode our experiences and also how we work with them.

Write from the shadow's perspective first. Let it speak in the first person. What has it been trying to tell you through your triggered reactions? What does it fear? What does it need from you? What wisdom does it carry that you've been dismissing?

Then respond with acceptance from your whole self. How might you honor both the shadow's concerns and your conscious values? What would integration look like rather than suppression or dominance?

Write it down, let it unfold without forcing resolution. You can write it as a dialogue if you want to see it more clearly.

Phase Five: Embodied Anchoring

Shadow work that remains purely cognitive doesn't create lasting change. Your body has been holding these patterns for years. Create a physical anchor for your new relationship with this shadow material. Design a simple gesture or posture that activates this integration in your conscious mind. This might be placing both hands on your heart to acknowledge both strength and vulnerability. It might be opening your palms to embody welcoming what you've rejected. It might be a specific breath pattern that signals wholeness.

While the shadow work is fresh, practice this gesture while visualizing the integration of the shadow.

Create a simple statement that goes with the gesture, for example: I am open to seeing the value in opposing ideas, even when I'm sure I'm right. Commit to doing this practice daily, especially when you notice the feeling activating. The dual practice of an embodied gesture linked with a specific mantra helps to rewire neural pathways more effectively than mental work alone.

Adaptations

Quick version (10 minutes): When triggered, ask only: "What quality am I reacting to?" and "Where does this exist in me?" Often this recognition alone loosens the grip.

Deep version (60+ minutes): Expand Phase Four into extended journaling. Let the dialogue continue across several pages. Ask the shadow what it looked like when it first formed. Explore its history in your life.

Three Shadows audit: Work through each shadow type systematically. What is your greatest strength and its blind spot? What wound still filters your perception? What quality do you judge that you might need?

Partner version: Share your trigger mapping with someone you trust. Ask them what patterns they see in your reactions that you might miss. Others often see our shadows more clearly than we do.

What to Expect

First few times: You may resist the Mirror Work phase. Seeing the quality you judge in yourself is uncomfortable. The dialogue may feel awkward or forced. The shadow may not want to speak or may speak with more intensity than expected. All of this is the practice working.

After a few times of doing the practice: You'll start noticing triggers in real-time, catching the reaction earlier in its arc. The dialogue becomes more natural. You may notice shadows that seemed separate are actually connected. The embodied anchor begins to work automatically, creating a pause for integration before reacting.

Common Obstacles

"I can't find this quality in myself." Look for the inverse or the compensation. If you judge passivity in others, you may be exhausting yourself with constant action. If you react to arrogance, you may be suppressing legitimate confidence. The shadow rarely looks identical to what triggers you. It's often a mirror image.

"The shadow material feels too big to work with." Start smaller. You don't have to integrate a lifetime of shadow in one session. Work with one trigger, one reaction, and one small piece. Shadow work is cumulative. Each session builds on the last.

Field Note

Stephen came to me because his coaching practice had stalled. He had been a respected teacher and a pioneer among his peers. Many of the people in his circle had been mentored by him at one time or another. He noticed that these same peers were now doing well in their work.

The problem he shared went like this: "I've taught most of these people a lot of what they know, and none of them reach out to offer referrals or share credit for my work as they're using it. It feels unjust."

We identified the trigger immediately as a sense of not feeling valued. When we looked at the shadow, it was clearly the shadow of wounds. His mentor had never valued his work, and after Stephen left, there was bitterness from his mentor about Stephen using techniques without paying homage. He had studied through apprenticeship, but his teacher had expectations of him becoming an employee rather than going out on his own.

As we stepped into the mirror practice, Stephen struggled with what the mirror was within his own behavior. In the end, he realized it was a sense of entitlement. He felt he deserved referrals and accolades for the work he had done. But when he looked back at his own training, it was the same situation. He had learned and then gone out on his own, which is naturally what happens when we mentor. This realization that he was carrying his mentor's shadow gave him clarity and an immediate sense of lightness.

As he dialogued with the shadow, he listened to its desire to be seen and valued. Holding that compassionately, he was able to see the other side. Underneath the entitlement was fear. Fear that he might not hold the value and skills he believed he did. Otherwise, why would his practice be stalling?

Once he owned this, the path forward became clear. He needed to re-enter the marketplace and share his gifts. His fear of not being valuable enough had generated a shadow of entitlement that kept him from facing a necessary growth edge around business development.

The integration had two steps. First, a question: Am I actually skilled? And if so, how would I know? As we reviewed the clients he had worked with and the people he had mentored, it became clear that his skills were highly developed. Owning that truth allowed him to step into the second question: How do I enter the marketplace in a way that lets me share these gifts more widely?

We used a standing posture called Bear for his anchor. Knees slightly bent, body upright, palms facing the chest. His anchor phrase was "sharing and curiosity."

When we followed up a few months later, Stephen had opened up to collaboration with his peers. He reached out to them with a new sense of appreciation for their skills. He developed partnerships that brought his work into the public and allowed him to learn from what his peers had developed along the way.

He told me he had been missing the learnings that were waiting for him once he released the shadow of entitlement. He was finally able to be the student of his students.

Remember This

The flashlight of focused attention illuminates specific targets with precision, while the moonlight of diffuse awareness reveals patterns and relationships that remain invisible under direct examination. Neither mode of seeing is superior. Each reveals different aspects of reality. The challenge is that our modern world overwhelmingly rewards flashlight perception, leaving us blind to what lies in the shadows beyond that beam.

Shadow material consists of those aspects of ourselves we've disowned, repressed, or pushed into unconsciousness. These aren't necessarily negative qualities but include any parts of ourselves that didn't receive approval or felt unsafe to express. What we don't own, owns us. Our shadows operate beneath the surface, influencing decisions and relationships in ways we don't recognize until we bring them into awareness.

The three shadows of leadership create predictable patterns. The shadow of strength emerges when our greatest capabilities prevent us from seeing other perspectives. The shadow of wounds manifests through unhealed experiences that create perceptual filters. The shadow of values appears when what we most strongly reject in others points to disowned aspects of ourselves. The Paradox of Illumination reveals that the brightest light often creates the darkest shadows: areas where we have the greatest clarity generate our most significant blind spots precisely because we never think to question them.

Shadow integration transforms not just individual leaders but entire systems. When we acknowledge our whole selves, including limitations and uncertainties, we create psychological safety that allows teams to surface collective blind spots. Energy previously spent on suppression becomes available for creative purpose. The practice reveals that what we thought was darkness contains unexpected gifts, expanding our range and effectiveness in ways that staying in the light never could.

11

YOUR NORTH STAR

"The two most important days in your life are the day you are born and the day you find out why."
— Author unknown

Well reader, congratulations. You've done significant work to get here.

Through the earlier chapters, you learned to listen deeply, tuning into the wisdom of body, mind, and intuition. You discovered how perception shapes reality, how the maps we inherit often lead us away from our authentic path. You explored the shadow territories where disowned parts of yourself waited for recognition. You practiced letting go, releasing attachment to outcomes and identities that no longer serve you. You learned to flow, balance, become still, recover, and consciously rewire your stress response.

All of these tools are for excavation. They are about clearing away the debris of conditioning, inherited expectations, and false perceptions to reveal a clearer and deeper connection to your essential self.

Now that the debris is cleared, what do we do next?

This chapter builds on that clarity by making choices about what matters to you, what's non-negotiable in how you want to walk your path.

One of the biggest challenges we face today is being overwhelmed with data, opinions, frameworks, and competing demands. Every significant decision seems to require more research, more analysis, and more consultation. We gather input until we are paralyzed by the abundance of data that's supposed to be helping us.

Meanwhile, life keeps moving. Decisions can't wait for a perfect answer. A colleague asks for your commitment on a project. An opportunity appears with a tight deadline. A crisis demands immediate response.

In these moments, the tools of analysis fail us. There is no time to weigh every variable, consult every expert, or model every outcome. Yet the decisions we make in these compressed moments often matter more than the ones we deliberate over for months.

What guides you when there is no time to think?

For most people, the honest answer is whatever happens to be loudest in that moment. Fear. Habit. The last opinion they heard. The path of least resistance. They make decisions reactively, then spend energy afterward justifying choices that were never really choices at all.

There's a better way.

Imagine having a handful of fixed coordinates so deeply internalized that they function like constellations in the night sky. No matter where you stand, no matter how disorienting your circumstances, you can look inward and instantly orient yourself. These coordinates don't tell you exactly how to get to where you're going. But they give you a clear direction, by checking in with who you are, and remembering what matters most. From that knowing, the path forward becomes clear.

These are your precepts. Your true north.

Precepts work because they operate at a different level than situational analysis. When you know your core values with clarity, you do not need to calculate every decision from scratch. You simply check: Does this action align with who I am? The answer comes quickly, almost instinctively, because you are not processing external variables. You are referencing internal truth.

This is not gut instinct in the casual sense. It is something more reliable. Your precepts are the distilled wisdom of everything you have learned about yourself through the work of these chapters. They are what remains after you have stripped away conditioning, confronted your shadows, and distinguished inherited maps from authentic direction.

The clients I work with who navigate complexity with apparent ease share this quality. They are not smarter or better informed than their struggling peers. They simply know their precepts. When pressure mounts and time compresses, they have coordinates to reference. Their decisions may not always be perfect, but they are consistent with who they are. And that consistency creates a kind of integrity that others recognize and trust.

You are ready to identify your own precepts now because you could not have done this work earlier. Before the shadow excavation, you might have named values that were actually inherited from family or culture. Before the perception work, you might have confused what you thought you should value with what you actually do. Before learning to let go, you might have clung to precepts that served an earlier version of yourself but no longer fit who you are becoming.

Timing matters. Precepts identified too early become another layer of conditioning. Precepts identified after some authentic self-examination become genuine navigation tools for your life.

By the end of this chapter, you will have identified your precepts. They will be there to guide you for the rest of your life.

This does not mean you must get them perfect on the first try. Everything that is alive is evolving to a more effective version of itself. Precepts are no different.

Precepts prove remarkably stable in their essence. But the way you understand and express them will deepen as you continue to apply them. A precept you name today might reveal new dimensions six months from now when you revisit it. Maybe you've moved through some deeper shadow content and can access another layer of self-discovery. The words you choose to express your precepts might sharpen after you've stress tested them through a few difficult situations and seen what held up and what didn't. Everything alive is always evolving; including our precepts.

Think of your first version as a strong draft, not a final engraving. The practices throughout this book are designed to be revisited. Each return reveals something the previous pass could not. Your precepts will evolve the same way. They will change and deepen with you.

The goal today is clarity sufficient for your navigation. It's your Beta version that you're testing. It's the ingredient you need to begin and refine as you grow.

Finding My Own Coordinates

After my time at the cancer center ended, the future was uncertain. The clinic had closed. I knew I would continue practicing medicine, but the question of where and how kept circling without resolution. Opportunities appeared, but none felt right. I wasn't looking for the easiest path or the most lucrative one. I wanted alignment. I just couldn't see the target.

So, I sat with the question: "What do I actually value?" Not what I thought I was supposed to value or what my training had told me to value. I let the experiences of those years at the cancer center speak to me without rushing toward answers.

Two realizations emerged that became the foundation of my precepts.

The first came from Jane.

Life is a gift, embrace it and teach others to do the same.

We lost a few patients at the clinic. That was the nature of the work. But Jane's death cut differently than the others for me. She was younger than me, more alive than most people I'd ever met, and she loved her life with a wholeness that was contagious. Watching her navigate her illness with such openness and then holding her hand as she crossed the threshold, something fundamental shifted in me.

Jane's death taught me about my own life. What a gift it is that we have time on this planet. How we spend each day is always an opportunity. For connecting with yourself. For showing up fully with the people around you. For walking your path with intention rather than drifting through it unconsciously.

Working with people who were fighting for every additional day, who wanted desperately to live, who grieved the future they would not see, I understood what I had been taking for granted in my own life. Their clarity about the value of being alive became my teacher. The reckless part of my life ended after that experience.

The second one was more obvious to me.

Develop and share tools for people to make their lives better.

I was here to bring tools to people so they could heal themselves. Not to be someone who solved problems for others, but someone who taught them to solve their own. Someone who helped them understand how their conscious and unconscious minds shaped their lives, contributing to either disease or health. My purpose was not to create dependence but capacity.

Developing tools to help others care for themselves evolved from medicine to working with individuals, leaders, and organizations. The precept evolved into the goal of amplification. These practices had transformed individual lives in my clinic and studio. What would happen if they could reach larger groups? What if consciousness and care and aligned action could spread beyond the people who happened to walk through my door?

The precepts lead me to the question: "What if I put myself inside a company?" Later the precepts would lead me to write this book.

Over the years, three more precepts joined these two.

What's most alive for me right now?

The third emerged from noticing what made me feel most alive. I am happiest when I'm exploring where others haven't been yet, discovering new information and ideas and putting them together in ways that are useful. There's a particular joy in bringing to light knowledge that might otherwise have remained hidden. This precept of curious exploration shapes how I approach every new challenge. It reminds me that my path requires venturing into unknown territory, not staying comfortable with what I already know.

The fourth came from the scientist in me.

Test it: Make sure it works.

I can't share information I haven't tested or vetted. It isn't enough for something to sound right or feel inspiring. I have to know that what I'm saying is true. True to my experience, true in the world, true in practice. This precept of integrity applies to everything I do and say. Every action, every teaching, every recommendation. If I haven't verified it, I don't pass it on as truth.

The fifth precept took the longest to articulate, though it had been operating in me for years before I found the words.

Love is the answer.

Love is at the heart of empathy, listening, care, and humility. It is my compass for making sure I meet every person with the consideration and openness they deserve. This precept of service through love keeps me honest about my motivations. Am I helping because it serves my ego, or because genuine care is flowing through me? The precept asks the question. My answer determines whether I'm aligned.

These five precepts have guided me through every significant decision since I identified them. They don't always make decisions pleasant, but they do make them clear. When I am living in alignment with them, joy, creativity, and connection flow naturally. These aren't things I have to chase. They emerge as byproducts of staying true to my coordinates.

What Your Precepts Are

A precept is not a goal. Goals are destinations. You reach them, celebrate, and set new ones. Precepts are navigational stars. They remain fixed in the sky while everything else shifts.

A precept isn't a rule. Rules are external constraints imposed on us. Precepts are internal commitments arising from our own clarity about who we are. Rules tell us what we cannot do. Precepts tell us who we are, and our actions flow from that knowing.

A precept is not an aspiration. Aspirations describe who you wish you were or hope to become. Precepts describe who you actually are when you are most aligned with yourself. The gap between aspiration and precept is the gap between who we are and who we're becoming. Aspirations live in the future. Precepts are the guides we use to get there.

Here is the test: Can you use it to make a decision when the answer isn't clear from the outside?

When someone offers you an opportunity and you have thirty seconds to respond, "I value relationships" doesn't help you choose. It's too abstract. But "I say yes to growth, even when it scares me" points you toward action. "I never trade integrity for convenience" draws a bright line.

Precepts work because they cut across every domain of your life. The same precept that guides how you show up in your marriage guides how you lead your team. The principle that shapes your relationship with yourself shapes your relationship with community. This is not compartmentalized wisdom. It is integrated truth about who you are.

Why five?

Three precepts are too few to capture the dimensionality of a human life. You will encounter situations where three coordinates leave you disoriented. Ten precepts are too many to hold in mind during moments of pressure. When you need them most, you won't be able to access them.

Five creates enough complexity to address real situations while remaining simple enough to function as a quick-check system. You can run a decision through five filters in seconds. You can remember five precepts under stress. You can teach five precepts to someone who needs to understand how you operate.

Think of your precepts as a rapid diagnostic. When confusion arises, when pressure mounts, when you feel pulled in competing directions, you ask five questions: Does this align with precept one? Precept two? Three, four, five? If the answer is yes across the board, you move forward with confidence. If any precept signals misalignment, you pause and examine more closely.

This is not a replacement for careful thinking. Complex decisions still deserve deliberation. But precepts give you a first filter that eliminates options quickly and highlights where to focus your attention. They also give you a foundation to return to when deliberation leads you in circles.

The precepts you identify in this chapter will appear throughout the remainder of this book. The final chapter's Compass practice integrates everything you've learned, and your precepts serve as the fixed coordinates around which everything else orients. You will also use them for the rest of your life.

Three Ways to Apply Your Precepts

Your precepts will serve you in three primary ways as you continue through this book and beyond.

The first is daily orientation. Each morning, before the noise of the day begins, you can reconnect with your coordinates. This doesn't require elaborate rituals. A simple reading of your five precepts or even holding them silently in mind for a moment reminds you who you are.

The second is decision-making. When choices arise, run them through your precepts. Does this opportunity align with all five? If yes, move forward with confidence. If one or more signals misalignment, pause. The misalignment doesn't necessarily mean no. It means look closer. Understand what the conflict is before you proceed.

The third is drift detection. Over time, without conscious attention, we all drift from our true north. Pressure accumulates. Compromises compound. One day you wake up and realize you've been living in misalignment for months without noticing. Your precepts give you a way to catch drift early. When something feels off but you can't name why, check your coordinates. Usually, the answer is there.

The practice that follows will guide you through identifying your own five precepts. Take your time with it. This is not a practice to rush through. The clarity you develop here will serve you for years.

Practice: Identifying Your Precepts

Applied Insights

The capacity to name and operate from your core values with clarity and consistency. This practice guides you to identify five precepts that serve as fixed coordinates for navigation, helping you make decisions under pressure, maintain alignment over time, and recognize when you've drifted from your true north.

When to Use

- As a foundational practice after completing the earlier chapters of this book
- When facing a major life transition or decision point
- When you sense you've been living by inherited values rather than your own
- When your actions consistently conflict with who you believe yourself to be
- As a periodic review to refine and deepen your relationship with your precepts

The Practice

Find 45—60 minutes of uninterrupted space with a journal. This practice requires writing.

Before you begin, take a few minutes to quiet your mind. Let your creativity flow. Keep your mind open, your heart open. The answers you're looking for aren't what others think you should be, but who you truly are and how you want to live.

Phase One: Exploration

Think about five people whose way of navigating life you deeply respect. These might be leaders, mentors, friends, historical figures, or even fictional characters. Each person should represent a quality you wish to embody.

Here's why this works: It's often easier to see a value clearly when it's embodied in someone else than to name it abstractly in yourself. The people you admire serve as mirrors. When you recognize a quality in them that resonates deeply, you are seeing something that already lives in you. The admiration is recognition. Like when you meet someone for the first time and it feels like you've known them forever.

For each person, identify the single value they most represent to you. Not a list of attributes, but the one essential principle/quality of their life that resonates. What is the core of why they made your list?

Write their name and the single value each one mirrors back to you.

Phase Two: Evidence from Your Life

Shift to your own experience. Recall three to five moments when you felt most aligned with yourself. Times when your actions matched your deepest sense of who you are. The scale doesn't matter. What matters is the felt-sense of rightness.

For each moment, write what made it feel aligned. What value were you honoring? What principle were you living?

Now recall three to five moments when you felt most out of alignment. Times when you acted against your own grain. When something felt wrong, even if you couldn't articulate why.

For each moment, write what value was transgressed. What value did you compromise? What would you have done differently if you had honored your true self?

The violations often reveal precepts more clearly than the alignments. We don't always notice when we're living in integrity. We almost always notice when we're not.

Phase Three: Ranking

Review everything you've written. The values mirrored by the people you admire. The principles present in your aligned moments. The values violated in your misaligned moments. Look for the threads that run through all of it.

Narrow your list down to five values that will represent your precepts. These are the fundamental qualities you want to always represent your true north.

Use these questions to get clarity:

If I am always aligned with this value, will it help me navigate difficult or confusing situations?

If I am always aligned with this value, will it help me achieve my goals?

If I am always aligned with this value, will it help me maintain alignment with who I am and want to be, both personally and professionally?

If a value doesn't pass all three questions, it may not be central or specific enough to be a precept. Remember we have lots of values, but only five precepts.

Phase Four: Expansion

Once you have your five values narrowed to single words or short phrases, expand each one. This is your deep dive into what this value means to you.

For each precept, write a few paragraphs on what it means to you personally and professionally, how you'll use it, and what benefit it will have in your life. Take your time. This expansion is where the precept becomes truly yours rather than an abstract concept. Push past the first layer of discovery and really dig into what it means to you. The more you write here, the better.

Phase Five: Distillation

Once you have all five expansions written, create a one-sentence statement for each that captures the essence of that deeper exploration. This sentence should serve as a quick reference that brings to mind all of the deeper meaning you explored in the previous phase.

Test your sentences: When you read each one, does it immediately connect you to the full meaning of that precept? If not, keep refining until it does.

Phase Six: Testing

Before finalizing, test your precepts against reality.

Think of a current decision you're facing. Run it through your five precepts. Does each one give you useful information? If a precept doesn't help you navigate real choices, it may be too abstract or may not actually be central to who you are.

Think of a past decision you regret. Would your precepts have helped you see the misalignment earlier? If not, something important may be missing from your list.

Think of a past decision you're proud of. Do your precepts capture why it was right? They should articulate what you already know in your bones.

Revise as needed. This testing often reveals that one or two precepts need sharpening or replacing.

Integration

Create a document that shows each precept word, then its one-sentence statement, then your expanded writing. Keep them together in a single place for reference.

Write your five precept words on a piece of paper and put them where you'll see them daily. On your wall, your whiteboard, or as a note on your phone. When confusion arises, look at your precepts and ask which one might be out of alignment. Usually, the answer is there.

Identify which of your five precepts will be most challenging to honor consistently. This is useful information. It points to where your growth edge lies.

Adaptations

Quick review version (15 minutes): If you've already identified your precepts, use this as a periodic check-in. Read each precept and its one-sentence statement. For each one, ask: Am I currently aligned? Where have I drifted? What needs attention?

Deep revision version (90+ minutes): After living with your precepts for several months, return to the full practice. Have any precepts shifted? Has your understanding deepened? Do the one-sentence statements still capture what matters? Update as needed.

Decision application version: When facing a specific decision, run it through each precept. Write what each precept says about this choice. Where do they align? Where is there tension? Let the precepts guide but not dictate.

What to Expect

First few times: You may struggle to narrow to five. Everything feels important. Or you may discover that values you thought were central don't pass the three questions. Phase Two violations may be uncomfortable to revisit. This discomfort is part of the clarification process.

After a few times of doing the practice: Your precepts become internalized reference points you can access quickly. You'll notice when you're drifting before the drift becomes serious. The precepts don't make decisions easier, but they make them clearer.

Common Obstacles

"I can't narrow to five." Look for overlap. Values that seem distinct often cluster around a deeper principle. "Honesty" and "authenticity" and "transparency" might all be expressions of a single precept about integrity. Find the root.

"My precepts feel too abstract to use." Return to Phase Five. The one-sentence statement should be specific enough to apply. "I value relationships" is too vague. "I protect my presence for what matters most" gives you something to work with.

Field Note

Eliza was moving from a role as a high-performing individual contributor into her first leadership position. She was good at listening, synthesizing ideas, and supporting others. But now she needed to do something that felt foreign to her: take up space in a room.

"I know how to contribute," she said. "I don't know how to lead a conversation. When there's a conflict, I freeze. I wait for someone else to resolve it."

We started by identifying her five precepts: transparent, receptive, curious, supportive, and decisive. As we worked through each one, a pattern emerged. Her values were heavily weighted toward openness and listening. Only one pointed toward action.

"What do you notice?" I asked.

She sat with it. "I've built my whole identity around responding. I don't know how to initiate effectively in a group."

This was her growth edge. Being receptive had served her well as an individual contributor. But leadership required her to also be decisive. To speak first sometimes. To name the conflict in the room rather than wait for someone else to do it.

We worked on integrating decisiveness with her other values. She didn't have to abandon her receptive nature. She could listen fully and then act. She could be curious and still move the group toward a decision. The values weren't in conflict. They needed to work together.

The shift came when she reframed what decisiveness meant. "Decisions are starting points," she said, "not final verdicts." This gave her permission to act without needing certainty. She could decide, learn, and adjust.

Over the following months, Eliza began guiding conversations rather than waiting for them to resolve on their own. She named tensions early. She offered her perspective before asking for others. Her team noticed. They told her she seemed more confident, more present.

She told me later that the breakthrough wasn't adding something new. It was letting a value she already held move from the background to the foreground.

Remember This

Precepts are navigational stars that remain fixed while everything else shifts. They tell you who you are so that action can flow from knowing rather than confusion. The test of a precept is whether it helps you make decisions under pressure. If it is too abstract to filter a real choice, it needs sharpening.

You could not have identified authentic precepts earlier in this book. The listening, perception, and shadow work were necessary preparation. Precepts named before that excavation risk being inherited values rather than genuine ones. The timing matters. Precepts identified too early become another layer of conditioning. Precepts identified after this depth of self-examination become genuine navigation tools.

Five precepts create enough complexity to address real situations while remaining simple enough to access under pressure. You can run a decision through five filters in seconds. Three is too few to capture the dimensionality of a human life. Ten is too many to hold in mind when you need them most.

Your precepts serve three functions: daily orientation before the noise begins, decision-making when choices arise, and drift detection when misalignment accumulates without your noticing. Think of your first articulation as a strong draft, not a final engraving. Precepts that emerge from genuine self-examination prove remarkably stable in essence, though the way you express them may evolve. The chapters that follow build on what you have established here. Your precepts are the fixed coordinates around which everything else orients.

12

FINDING RHYTHM

"Forget not that the earth delights to feel your bare feet, and the winds long to play with your hair."
— Kahlil Gibran

Morning arrives gradually. Light increases before the sun appears. Birds begin moving before warmth returns. The day starts changing long before we notice it has changed.

We tend to measure progress as forward motion, but most movement in nature happens through return. Growth rises, peaks, declines, and begins again. The daily passage from morning to night mirrors the year from winter to summer. The moon moves from new to full and back again. Careers and relationships follow the same pattern: expansion, stability, and eventually transformation. Life moves in cycles, not straight lines.

Nothing in the natural world tries to remain at its peak. Birds depart before the cold arrives. Whales cross entire oceans on invisible calendars. Trees release their leaves in response to shortening light and falling temperatures. The soil rests long before the next growth appears. Each participates fully in its season, then transitions without resistance. Humans alone attempt to operate at peak output year-round. When we remain out of sync with our cycles for too long, the body or the situation initiates correction. The project stalls, motivation disappears, priorities rearrange themselves. What appears as disruption often functions as a return to alignment.

This rhythm sits at the center of Daoist philosophy and Chinese medicine. The Daoist concept of Wu Wei, often translated as "effortless action," describes trusting the unseen ordering that moves through things when you stop forcing the moment. Alignment shows up in life as timing. You act when the way opens and refrain when the way is still forming. As the Dao De Jing reminds us, *One who tries to control everything will lose it. One who lets life unfold will find its depth.* It is discernment and skillful timing: knowing when to act and when to rest, when to push forward and when to pull back.

This connects directly to what we explored in the flow chapter. Just as water finds its path without forcing, our energy ebbs and flows through cycles. Fighting these rhythms by trying to maintain constant peak performance is like rowing against the tide. It creates resistance and drains resources without moving us forward.

The Science of Natural Rhythms

Modern science has confirmed what sacred traditions have always known: our bodies operate according to multiple biological rhythms. Circadian rhythms govern our daily cycles of sleep, hormones, body temperature, and cognitive function. Ultradian rhythms move in waves of about ninety minutes, shifting us between focused attention and more diffuse, integrative thinking. Infradian rhythms span weeks and months, shaping mood, energy, and creativity across longer arcs.

Understanding these rhythms changes how you structure your life.

Circadian rhythm creates natural peaks and valleys of energy throughout the day. Most people experience their sharpest focus in the late morning and a dip in the early afternoon. If you're doing deep strategy work at 2:30pm every day and wondering why it feels like mud, you're fighting your physiology. Working with this pattern means protecting high-energy windows for demanding work and using the valleys for routine tasks or genuine rest.

Ultradian rhythm shows that focused work moves in waves of around ninety minutes. After that, the brain needs a shift — not distraction, but recovery: movement, stillness, or a change of environment. Pushing through when the body is asking for a change does not create more productivity; it creates depletion.

Infradian rhythms ask for attention across longer spans. The most natural frame for observing them is the ninety-day season. Each season carries its own arc of energy, and within that arc you move through recognizable phases that repeat year after year.

Start by tracking simple markers through one full season. Note your energy levels each week: are you waking easily or struggling? Does the afternoon feel sustainable or depleted? Track creative patterns: when do ideas arrive, and when does execution feel easier than ideation? Notice social rhythms: craving connection or solitude? Pay attention to the body: when illness appears, sleep needs change, or exercise feels nourishing versus draining.

As you track, each season reveals an internal rhythm. Spring energy builds after the equinox toward the fullness of the summer solstice. Summer peaks, then gradually turns inward as days shorten. Autumn carries the momentum of release toward winter stillness. Winter reaches its deepest point at the solstice and begins regenerating toward spring.

Within each season, your energy tends to rise and fall along a similar curve. Early spring brings excitement, late spring confidence. Early winter offers rest, late winter anticipation. After four seasons you begin to see a personal annual rhythm. Strategic thinking may sharpen in autumn when refinement is strong. Creative output may expand in late spring as energy builds. January may consistently require protection for rest after the holidays. These are not random fluctuations, but your body's relationship with cycles of light and time that have shaped human biology for millennia.

Once recognized, you can plan accordingly. Schedule demanding projects when your Infradian rhythm supports peak output and protect your quieter seasons for integration and recovery. Your annual rhythm becomes information, creating the same ease as honoring daily peaks and ninety-minute focus cycles.

When we ignore these rhythms and try to operate at peak output year-round, burnout follows. It's like planting in the same field without rotating the crops or having a fallow season. The soil loses nutrients, becomes depleted, and production steadily declines.

This science reinforces what we explored in the stillness chapter: those moments of apparent non-productivity are part of the cycle, creating the conditions for insight and discovery that constant activity prevents.

The Cyclical Wisdom of Chinese Medicine

In Chinese medicine, the understanding of rhythmic cycles extends beyond the body to the relationship between humans and the natural world. The Wu Xing, or Five Phase theory, describes how energy transforms through five elements: Wood, Fire, Earth, Metal, and Water. Each represents a stage in the cyclical movement of Qi.

These five phases correlate with seasons, organs, emotions, and stages of development.

Wood corresponds to spring, representing new growth and visionary planning. This is the energy of beginning — tender shoots pushing through soil, ideas taking their first form.

Fire connects to summer, embodying full expression and joyful connection. This is peak energy, maximum output, and the time when everything planted comes into full bloom.

Earth represents the transitions between seasons, offering grounding and integration. It is the pause between phases, the moment of centering before the next movement begins.

Metal aligns with autumn, the time of refinement, and letting go. Harvest energy but also release. The tree drops its leaves not from weakness but from wisdom.

Water embodies winter, the phase of deep stillness and potential. Nothing appears to be happening, yet beneath the surface essential regeneration occurs.

Consider your own life right now. Which phase are you in? Not the phase you wish you were in, or the one you believe you should be in, but the one that is actually present. What is that phase asking of you that you might be resisting?

In my Chinese medicine practice, I observed how disharmony often results from resistance to the natural cycle. Patients who refused to rest during their personal "winter" phases developed deeper imbalances. Those who could not let go during "autumn" accumulated stagnation that prevented new growth. The medicine was never about forcing change. It was about recognizing where someone was in their cycle and supporting alignment with that phase.

The same principle applies to you. The question is not how to change the season you are in, but whether you are willing to recognize it and align with your natural rhythm. This does not require abandoning responsibility. It is a way of optimizing your energy and prioritizing your time and actions with clarity.

Integration with Shadow Work

Our relationship with life's rhythms often contains shadow material. Many of us carry unconscious beliefs about rest, productivity, and the "right" way to use our time.

Common shadows include the belief that rest equals laziness or weakness. Fear that slowing down means falling behind. Attachment to identity based on constant productivity. Difficulty letting go of completed phases. Resistance to stepping into new challenges.

My own shadow around cycles emerged clearly during my recovery. I had to confront my fear of becoming irrelevant if I was not constantly doing. I had to recognize that my resistance to winter phases in my life was connected to my fear of the ultimate winter.

The most difficult shadow I faced was the identity I had built around being the "teacher" and the "healer." In those roles I was placed on a pedestal. I would always be strong. Always healthy. Always aligned. Over time I internalized those expectations and made them part of who I was. I believed I was living in balance, that I would always have the resources to meet every demand.

That belief had to soften.

We all experience misalignment. Alignment practices exist so we can recognize when we have drifted and return to balance. They are not about perfection; they are about awareness.

Letting go of those identities allowed me to begin learning again. As I integrated these shadows, I found a deeper acceptance that I would lose my way at times — and that this, too, was part of the cycle. With that acceptance came a greater capacity to embrace every phase of my life's rhythms, including the ones I once resisted.

What identity have you built that depends on constant expansion? What would it mean to let that identity rest, even temporarily?

Shadow integration connects directly to boundaries and limits. The boundaries between seasonal phases aren't limitations but essential borders that, like the banks of a river, channel energy and create the conditions for healthy growth and natural movement.

Tree Wisdom

Consider how a tree moves through the seasons. In spring, it channels energy into new growth, leaves unfurling, and branches extending. In summer, it operates at full capacity, capturing sunlight and producing fruit. In autumn, it lets go of what it no longer needs, directing energy inward. In winter, though appearing dormant, it consolidates strength in its roots, preparing for the next cycle of growth.

At no point does the tree resist its current season or try to remain in perpetual summer. Its wisdom lies in complete participation in whatever season it currently experiences.

The tree understands its nature. Its goal is to reach down into the earth, with roots seeking moisture and nutrients, while its leaves stretch toward sunlight, creating oxygen and using carbon to grow taller, to bear fruit or seeds, and to generate new life. If a seed sprouts on the angled side of a creek bed, its roots will reach through that creek bed into the earth, and its trunk will grow and bend to point its leaves toward the sky. The tree may appear crooked, curved, and bent. But in its "crookedness," it will be beautiful and aligned with its nature. Being aligned with nature creates the most harmonious and fruitful existence.

This is the essence of living in harmony with seasonal rhythms. Not imposing our ideal of how things "should" be, but instead recognizing and aligning with the natural flow of each system in which we participate. Just as each breath moves through its own seasons of inhalation and exhalation, our lives thrive when we honor the natural alternation between expansion and contraction, between doing and being, between manifesting and resting.

Seasonal Wisdom

Through consistent practice and patient observation, you'll develop seasonal discernment: the ability to recognize and align with the natural cycles in all aspects of your life. Like the tree that grows in perfect harmony with its seasons, you'll learn to achieve your goals not through constant force but through intelligent alignment with the rhythms that already exist. By bringing conscious attention to the rhythms already operating within and around you, you can begin to align more skillfully with life's natural cycles.

The gift of understanding seasonal rhythm isn't just in the efficiency it brings to our efforts, but in the way it teaches us to live. Responsive rather than reactive. Powerful yet flexible. Always moving forward while remaining true to our essential nature. As you continue to explore and apply these principles, you'll discover that the most sustainable success comes not from perpetual doing but from the harmonious dance with the seasons that mirror the natural rhythms of life.

Practice: The Rhythm Map

Applied Insights

The capacity to recognize where you are in natural cycles and align with what each phase asks rather than fighting against it. This practice trains you to see time as cyclical rather than linear, mapping the seasons operating simultaneously at different scales of your life. Over time, you develop the ability to work with available energy rather than forcing what isn't there.

When to Use

- When you feel exhausted despite adequate rest
- When you're pushing hard but results aren't coming

- When something feels off but you can't name why
- When entering a new phase of work, relationship, or life
- When you sense you're fighting against a natural rhythm
- As a periodic check-in to realign with what's actually happening

The Practice

Find 20-30 minutes of quiet space with paper or a journal. Pick a particular aspect of your life to focus on: a project, a relationship, your career path, or your health. Frame the question like this: What season am I in with this, and what do I need to do to align with this phase?

You'll look at this focus from multiple viewpoints, from daily rhythms to life stages, to see where you're aligned with natural energy and where you're forcing something that isn't there.

Phase One: Understanding the Seasons

The same pattern that moves through a year moves through a month, a week, a day, a project, a career, and a life. Winter's rest and reflection gives way to spring's emergence and drive, summer's full expression and connection, then autumn's harvest and release, before returning to winter.

Before mapping one of your own rhythms, understand what each season asks:

Winter asks for rest, reflection, and patience with apparent emptiness. Winter says: stop pushing, allow stillness, trust that spring will come.

Spring asks for courage to begin, readiness to push hard and grow, and energy for experimentation. Spring says: try things, expect mistakes, celebrate failure and growth.

Summer asks for sustained engagement, full expression, and celebration of abundance. Summer says: give your all, share your gifts, celebrate with others.

Autumn asks for honest evaluation, gratitude for harvest, and conscious release of what's complete. Autumn says: acknowledge achievements, release attachments, prepare for rest.

Phase Two: Mapping Your Current Seasons

Look at the situation from multiple viewpoints and go straight into the four scales (daily cycle, work/creative cycle, relationships, life stage). Frame the question like this: What season am I in with this project and what do I need to do to align with this phase?

Your daily cycle: Where are you in today's rhythm? Dawn corresponds to spring energy. Morning moves into summer. Afternoon shifts toward autumn. Evening and night enter winter.

Your work or creative cycle: What phase is your current main focus in? Ideation and incubation are winter. Early development is spring. Full production is summer. Completion and evaluation is autumn.

Your relationships: What season are your important connections experiencing? New relationships are spring. Established partnerships in full expression are summer. Relationships ready for evolution are autumn. Relationships in transition are winter.

Your life stage: What season of life are you in? Not your chronological age, but your felt sense of where you stand in your own journey.

Write which season you're in at each scale for the question you are mapping.

Phase Three: Reading the Overlaps

Now look at what you've mapped. You might be in the morning spring of your day while experiencing the autumn of a project. You could be in life's winter while your career experiences summer.

Notice where seasons align across scales. When multiple cycles are in summer simultaneously, energy is abundant, but burnout risk is high. When multiple cycles are in winter, rest is essential, but productivity expectations may create conflict.

Notice where seasons conflict. A project demanding summer productivity while you're in life's winter creates tension. A relationship asking for spring vulnerability while your work is in autumn's release can feel disorienting.

Write what you notice about how your seasons interact.

Phase Four: Alignment Assessment

Honestly assess where you're aligned with or fighting these natural rhythms.

Where are you trying to force summer productivity during winter's call for rest?

Where are you resisting spring's invitation to begin with courage and conviction?

Where are you clinging when autumn asks for release?

Where are you avoiding winter's necessary stillness?

Name the place where you're most strongly fighting what a season is asking.

Phase Five: One Alignment

From your assessment, choose one specific way you could honor what the seasons are asking of you while you look at your question.

If you're in winter but forcing summer: What would rest look like today? What could you stop pushing?

If you're resisting spring: What small beginning could you allow? What first step have you been avoiding?

If you're fighting autumn: What needs to be released? What are you holding past its time?

Write one concrete action that aligns with your season.

Adaptations

Quick version (5 minutes): Ask only: "What season am I in with my primary focus right now?" and "Am I fighting or flowing with what it asks?" Adjust one thing accordingly.

Deep version (60+ minutes): Map every significant domain of your life. Journal about your history with each season. Which do you resist most? Which do you rush through? Where did you learn to fight natural rhythms?

Daily check-in version: Each morning, note which season you're in at one consistent scale. This regular recognition helps you align before resistance creates exhaustion.

Weekly review version: At week's end, assess which seasons shifted, where you aligned well, and where you fought. Use this to set an intention for the coming week.

What to Expect

First few times: You may struggle to identify which season you're in, especially if you've been fighting rhythms for a long time. The concept of winter as valuable rather than something to push through may feel foreign. You may discover you've been in one season far longer than you realized.

After a few times of doing the practice: You'll start recognizing seasonal shifts as they happen rather than after misalignment forces awareness. The friction of fighting rhythms becomes more obvious, and alignment becomes more natural. You'll develop patience with winter and willingness to release in autumn.

Common Obstacles

"I don't have the luxury of honoring seasons. I have to produce." The seasons don't stop because you ignore them. Fighting winter doesn't create summer. It creates depletion. Even small alignments help. You can't always change your schedule, but you can change how you hold what you're doing.

"Everything feels like winter." Extended winter often signals that something deeper needs attention. Return to the Oasis Map or the Precepts practice. Winter that never ends may be depression, burnout, or profound misalignment rather than natural rhythm.

Field Note

Mira was a COO at a company she had been with since its inception. She had been working around the clock, either raising money, helping to build products, organizing the teams, or selling the product. It was standard practice to wear many hats when starting companies from scratch. Over four years she had helped build the company's teams, operations, and infrastructure. The company was growing, but she was exhausted.

We looked at the seasons of the company, the team, and her time there. It was clear that the company was still in its spring phase. Building and tuning the products to be of value to the market. Still growing and upskilling the teams. Working toward profitability in the long run.

The next phase of growth was going to require a huge push, but Mira had realized that she was in an autumn phase. She needed to let go and recharge. The company was stable enough, and she felt ready to move on. For her, the initial building phase was always her favorite space to work in. Once the foundation was built and the course had been plotted, her interest started to wane.

It became clear that it was time for her to leave the company, and so she did. She left on good terms, with ownership and a severance that gave her time to figure out what was next.

Now realigned, she felt clear. But about a month after leaving, having rested and recharged, she started getting restless. She wanted to start doing something. Her sense of value was based in action and accomplishment, and she started jumping into other projects to release the tension she was feeling.

For Mira, being in a state of reflection for too long without action felt like navel gazing. As we talked about what was next for her, I asked her to spend some more time in this winter phase of being between roles. She reluctantly agreed to dig deeper into the season of life and career and what information that might yield.

First, she created an inventory of her professional life: her experiences, failures, and successes. Then we began to look at what she had done that had brought her the most satisfaction and joy. She was in her early fifties, which she felt was the summer of her life and also the summer of her career. This meant she was ready to step into roles that would value all of her skills, wisdom, and connections in her field.

When she reframed her search based on this, she ruled out roles that didn't align with her seasons. This filter allowed only the most aligned roles that would recognize her gifts and be able to make the most out of them. She ended up in a fractional CEO role, sitting on the board of two companies, and began writing her first book. This allowed her to stay in roles where her creativity and starter mindset could be combined with her skills and relationships, all without demanding sixteen-hour days.

When I asked her what had shifted, she said, "I stopped trying to find a job. I started asking what truly mattered to me in this season. Once I knew that, the right roles found me."

Remember This

Life moves in cycles, not lines. The same pattern that carries a year through winter, spring, summer, and autumn moves through a single day, a project, a career, and a life itself. When we fight against these natural rhythms by trying to maintain perpetual summer, we create the conditions for burnout, diminished creativity, and ultimately failure.

Your body operates according to multiple biological rhythms that influence everything from energy to creativity. Circadian rhythms govern your daily cycles of alertness and rest. Ultradian rhythms move in ninety-minute waves between focused attention and diffuse thinking. Infradian rhythms span days or months, affecting mood and creative capacity across longer arcs. Working with these rhythms means protecting your high-energy windows for demanding work, honoring the ninety-minute need for recovery, and tracking your patterns across weeks and months to recognize what your body already knows.

The Five Phases of Chinese medicine offer a framework for reading these cycles at any scale. Wood energy initiates and plans. Fire energy expresses and connects. Earth energy grounds and integrates. Metal energy refines and releases. Water energy rests and regenerates. The question is not which phase you prefer, but which phase you are actually in, and what that phase is asking of you that you might be resisting.

The tree offers the clearest teaching. It channels energy into new growth in spring, operates at full capacity in summer, releases what it no longer needs in autumn, and consolidates strength in its roots through winter. At no point does it resist its current season or try to remain in perpetual summer. The gift of seasonal wisdom is learning to do the same: responsive rather than reactive, powerful yet flexible, always moving forward while remaining true to your essential nature.

13

THE THRESHOLD

"Airplanes are safest when they are on the ground,
but that's not what airplanes are made for."
— Unknown

There is a moment in every journey of growth when knowledge has to become action. When understanding has to transform into embodiment. This moment comes as an unmistakable threshold that requires us to choose between remaining in familiar territory or stepping onto an unknown path. Like airplanes built for flight, yet safest on the ground, we are designed for something greater than the security of the familiar.

The difference between those who actually create change and those who just accumulate knowledge lies in their willingness to cross the threshold from safety to action.

You have been gathering tools throughout this book. The Three-Channel Listening has shown you how to tune into the wisdom of body, mind, and intuition. The boundary work has taught you how to create containers for growth. The shadow integration has revealed hidden aspects of yourself waiting to be reclaimed. But theory alone accomplishes nothing. Change begins when you decide to step through the doorway of commitment to practice. You can read about swimming forever, but until you get in the water, you can't learn to swim. The magic is in the practice. Until you try, fail, learn, and try again with your new learnings, you don't build and refine your skills.

I like to ride motorcycles. They have always shown me my skills and taught me my limits. Having ridden since youth, then taking an eighteen-year break when my children were born, I returned to riding a few years ago with a new view. In my younger days, riding meant pushing every limit of my senses, matching my skills to a fast-changing, unpredictable environment. It was one of my earliest experiences of immersive focus. There is no room for the mind to wander when you're leaning into a corner at eighty miles an hour. Later I found that same quality of focus in meditation, holding a singular intent in my mind's eye with no distraction. The motorcycle taught me what meditation later refined: complete immersion in practice, whether on two wheels or on a meditation cushion, requires complete commitment and focus.

This threshold appears differently for each person. For some, it's a career transition that requires leaving behind decades of accumulated expertise. For others, it appears as the decision to address patterns that have limited their relationships for years. In organizations, it might present itself as the moment when a team must abandon familiar but outdated processes to embrace new ways of working. Regardless of its specific form, the threshold always carries the same essential quality: it requires you to release your attachment to who you have been in order to become who you are capable of being.

The Architecture of Resistance

Resistance is how we find the door we need to open in order to step into a new stage of growth. Before we can cross any threshold, we need to move through our resistance. Sometimes it's as simple as deeply knowing where you're going. And sometimes it's as complicated as moving through deeply ingrained programming that began early in your life and has left you with misperceptions that you carry in your body without consciously realizing it. Resistance reflects the shadow, and we need to bring light and understanding to what's next. Resistance operates on three distinct layers, and each layer speaks a different language.

The first layer of resistance is physical. Your body holds patterns that predate your conscious decision to change. The executive who decides to delegate more and finds their nervous system flooding with anxiety. The chest tightens, breathing shallows; hands reach for the phone to check on delegated projects. This isn't a weakness or failure. It's the body speaking in the only language it knows, sensation and impulse, trying to protect you from a danger it learned about long before this situation.

This physical resistance is the entry point. When you notice your body resisting what your mind has decided, you've found exactly where your work begins. The body often holds shadow material; old programs running beneath conscious awareness. A tech leader's compulsive checking might trace back to a startup failure where inattention proved catastrophic. Our bodies store the lesson that hypervigilance means survival. Until you listen to what your body is trying to protect you from, you won't be able to override the programming. It's hard to do anyway, but without understanding it always fails.

The practice here is simple but not easy: slow down enough to hear what the body is saying. Where is the tension? What does it want you to know? What earlier experience taught your nervous system this particular fear? The resistance isn't an obstacle to your transformation. It's your first teacher, pointing directly to what needs attention.

The second layer of resistance is mental and emotional. This is where our minds create elaborate justifications for why now isn't the right time. *The conditions aren't perfect. We need more information. We should wait until after this project, this quarter, this year.* These thoughts feel rational, but they're usually irrational fear wearing the mask of prudence.

Emotional resistance hides inside these rational-sounding objections. We tell ourselves we're being strategic when we're actually being protective. The skill here is learning to parse the facts from the emotional content, to recognize when "I need more data" actually means "I'm afraid of what happens if this doesn't work." When you can name the emotion beneath the mental resistance, you create space for an honest dialogue and a conscious choice.

The third layer is relational. We exist within webs of relationships that have organized themselves to reinforce who we've been. When we start to change, these systems push back. Not from malice, but from a need for the stability of the familiar. The leader who starts setting boundaries finds their team confused by the new unavailability. The executive who expresses a newfound vulnerability encounters discomfort from colleagues who don't know how to respond to this new behavior.

Every person in our lives functions as a mirror, reflecting back aspects of ourselves and our choices to each other. These mirrors reinforce each other's identities, just like the mirror we check before we leave the house. But mirrors are also biased. They carry their own viewpoints, their own stories, their own investments in who you are. A mirror that shows you something uncomfortable might be revealing your growth edge, or it might be revealing their discomfort with your growth. Learning to read these relational signals without being attached to them requires understanding the biases each one carries. We do this without realizing it already. Imagine you feel deflated after your boss just slammed you. Who do you reach out to? That's right, you already have someone in mind. They are the person who's going to give you the answer you need at that moment.

The path to consciously move through all three layers of resistance follows the same principles: Your body speaks through sensation. Your mind speaks to you through thoughts and feelings. Your relationships speak through your actions. Each layer of resistance contains information about where you're attached, where your perception might be distorted, where surrender might serve you better than force. The resistance isn't blocking your path. It's showing you where your work is.

The Upper Limit Problem

There's a particular form of resistance that emerges precisely when we stand at the threshold of expansion. In his book *The Big Leap,* Gay Hendricks calls it the Upper Limit Problem. His research reveals that we each carry an energetic thermostat for how much success, happiness, and fulfillment we can handle experiencing, before we do something to sabotage it. When we exceed this setting, we unconsciously create situations to bring ourselves back down to a more contracted but familiar zone.

This pattern shows up in leadership all the time. When a company hits a new gear of profit and growth, there's a new way of operating required. Expansion demands scaling, delegation, up-leveling talent, and investing in team members' growth. Bigger risks need to be taken to adapt to the new circumstances.

The same is true for individual expansion when we step into the possibility of the life we are meant to live. The relationship we've always wanted. The dream job. A whole new phase of self-discovery and growth. We often spend years seeking this more expanded way of living and operating, personally and professionally. But once we arrive at that transformation, once we've crossed that threshold, we need to build awareness and infrastructure to stay in that expanded state.

What often happens instead: expansion is followed by contraction. A desire to revert to the familiar instead of building new skills to grow into the larger framework. Identifying that contraction, working through it, and recognizing the places where we might be undermining ourselves is critical to stepping into our highest potential.

But why does this contraction happen?

Hendricks frames it this way: when we move into a larger and more expansive state of consciousness and fulfillment, discomfort comes with it because we are in a larger environment where our normal touchstones for identifying who we are and where we're going are not as readily available. Imagine moving from a one-bedroom apartment where you felt restricted on bad days and protected on good days, into a ten-room mansion with floor-to-ceiling windows and open-concept design. On a good day, that expansiveness gives you a sense of freedom. On a day where you feel unsure of yourself, that same expansiveness can make you feel lost.

We've all watched this pattern from the outside. The executive at the height of their career who has an affair that destroys their marriage. The founder who picks an unwinnable fight that tanks the company they built. The artist who finally gets recognition and then disappears into addiction. I've watched billion-dollar deals fall apart because one side gets stuck on a $100,000 item. From the outside it looks like self-destruction. From the inside, it's our unconscious drive to return to a familiar zone. The same principle applies to any form of expansion. We need to develop the skills and capacity to operate in our new, larger space.

Think about your own life. Where have you experienced expansion followed by an urge to contract? Maybe you finally got the promotion and immediately started doubting whether you deserved it. Professional athletes all talk about going through this time of failing performance after they've achieved the highest accolades in their sport. The ones who make it through tell a story of building new skills to keep their minds clear and manage the expectations that come after having achieved so much. They usually find their way back to the reason they love to play the game.

Where is your thermostat set? And what would it take to keep it there long enough to build the capacity to stay?

The Power of Clear Intent

You're house hunting with your partner. Same house. Same tour. You walk out and you've seen two completely different properties.

You saw the cracked foundation, the outdated electrical, the way the neighbors' houses are too close. You're calculating repair costs and resale value. Your partner saw the light coming through the kitchen windows, the built-in bookshelves, and the backyard perfect for summer dinners. They're already imagining where the furniture goes.

Neither of you is wrong. You're just looking with different intents.

Your intent is security. You need to know this house won't become a money pit, that you're making a sound investment, that you can trust the decision. That intent acts like a search beam that illuminates structural integrity, financial risk, and long-term value.

Your partner's intent is home. They're looking for the feeling of belonging, for space that invites the life they want to live, for the rightness of place. That intent highlights possibility, atmosphere, and potential.

Intent shapes what becomes visible. It's not passive. It actively constructs your reality by directing what you notice, what you remember, what you think matters.

This happens everywhere. The team meeting where someone suggests a new approach and half the room immediately sees obstacles while the other half sees opportunity. The performance review where your manager lists three things you're doing well and one thing to improve, and you only hear the one criticism.

Your intent in each moment determines what data reaches your conscious awareness. If your intent is to avoid being exposed, you can't see the learning opportunity. If your intent is proving you were right, you can't hear the valid feedback. If your intent is maintaining control, you miss the chance to develop your team's capacity.

The catch is that most of us aren't consciously choosing our intent. We're operating on automatic intents shaped by fear, past experience, or emotional charge. The executive whose intent got set to "protect my reputation" after one public failure. The leader whose intent is locked into "don't get hurt again" after a betrayal. These intents keep running in the background, filtering your world. You think you're seeing reality when you're seeing one narrow slice filtered through old protective programming.

When your intent isn't clear, you drive past opportunities without registering them. They're there, visible to someone who knows what they're looking for, but invisible to you. And when your intent is too narrow, you might see only one type of solution while screening out what you actually need.

In quantum physics, the observer changes everything. Before observation, a particle exists in what's called superposition. This is when a particle exists in multiple possible states simultaneously. The act of measurement collapses these possibilities into one actuality. Something similar happens with Intent and commitment. Before you get clear on what you want, multiple futures exist in simultaneous possibilities. The moment you bring focused intent to bear, one path crystallizes while others fade. That's why we know that being honest with yourself about what you want in life is so critical to receiving it.

In the Upper Limit Problem, when your thermostat is set low, you literally cannot see the opportunities that would take you beyond your familiar zone. They're there, just like the praise your boss was giving you during your review, but your filters are tuned to a smaller life and so you only see the criticism. Expanding your thermostat isn't just about tolerating more success. It's about being able to perceive possibilities that were previously invisible to you.

The practical implication is this: Clear intent always precedes opportunity. Not because the universe magically rearranges itself around your desires, but because your clear intent changes what you're capable of noticing, receiving, and acting on. The work isn't to manifest a different reality. The work is to become clear enough that you can finally see what was always available.

What would become visible to you if you got truly clear about what you wanted?

Jumping Off the Cliff

Twenty years ago in Mexico, standing at the edge of a cliff above a cenote filled with turquoise water, I learned something essential about the nature of commitment that has informed my work ever since. What seemed like a manageable thirty-foot drop from the water's edge transformed into something that appeared impossibly high once I stood at the precipice. Every step up the cliff path had increased the distance from the water and the distance I felt from my initial confidence.

This experience mirrors what happens when we approach significant life transformations. From a distance, change seems manageable, even exciting. We can see the benefits clearly: the sense of accomplishment, the growth, the new possibilities. As we get closer to the actual moment of commitment, the magnitude of what we are undertaking becomes real. The theoretical becomes actual. The abstract becomes immediate. Initially jumping into the water looked fun, and lots of people were doing it. But with every few steps I hiked up alongside the cliff; the water got farther away. I felt my anxiety increase with every step.

Standing on that cliff, I had to confront a fundamental question: Would I let fear stop me from doing something I wanted to experience? I had climbed the cliff with intention. I had assessed the risks and found them acceptable. The only thing standing between me and the experience was my willingness to take the last step.

The moment of jumping taught me something that years of meditation practice had only approximated: Stillness and peace always accompany total commitment. Once we commit fully, all other options collapse into one, just like the subatomic particle in physics. Everything becomes one single point of clarity. Once I stepped off the cliff, all the mental noise, the calculating, the hesitation vanished. There was only the present moment, only the experience itself. The transformation hit the moment I committed. It was terrifying and amazing, and I felt camaraderie with the other jumpers and a new level of belief in my ability to do things that seemed impossible.

This jump became my model for the last step of commitment in anything I do. Until I took the last step, until I committed, I had not entered true commitment. From then on, I could handle any question, no matter how difficult, by asking myself: Am I taking this last step?

Commitment as Daily Practice

Commitment is a capacity we develop through practice. Just as we build physical strength through progressive training, we build commitment capacity through increasingly significant acts of follow-through. Each time we step into commitment, especially when we are feeling resistance, we strengthen our ability to commit to more challenging growth in the future. This is how we move through obstructions like the Upper Limit Problem.

This process begins with micro-commitments. These are small, daily promises we make to ourselves that might seem insignificant but serve as the foundation for larger transformations. The commitment to spend five minutes in morning stillness. The commitment to engage in a hard conversation when it arises. The commitment to pause before reacting when triggered. These micro-commitments train our brains, helping us to forge new, stronger neural pathways. Remember that thought initiates neurons to fire, and when they fire together, they wire together.

When someone cannot say no to requests, they frequently fail to honor their commitments, eroding both credibility and self-trust. The solution often begins with a single micro-commitment: pausing for three breaths before responding to any request for time. This simple practice creates space to access the Three-Channel Listening. The body signals through tension when a request does not align with priorities. Emotional intelligence recognizes when motivation comes from fear rather than enthusiasm. Intuition offers clarity about what deserves a yes, and what doesn't. Your clarity in that moment creates clarity for the other people involved in the question. Clarity releases psychological noise for the whole group, creating a free flow of energy.

Over time, micro-commitments transform into a comprehensive practice of conscious commitment. We learn to make fewer but more powerful commitments, following through with consistency that rebuilds trust with ourselves and others. The threshold that needs crossing is incremental, built through daily practice rather than a single leap.

Our bodies know when we are ready to commit, often before our minds catch up. Each of us has specific physical signatures that indicate alignment or misalignment with a potential commitment. For some, alignment appears as a sense of expansion in the chest, deeper breathing, or groundedness in the lower body. Misalignment might manifest as constriction in the throat, tension in the shoulders, or feeling fatigued and pulled backward. These somatic signals offer information that transcends rational analysis.

Learning to read these signals requires practice and patience. Our bodies have been conditioned by years of overriding their wisdom in favor of mental logic or external expectations. The executive who has learned to ignore exhaustion in pursuit of achievement needs time to recalibrate their sensitivity to physical signals. The leader who has suppressed emotional responses to appear strong must gradually rebuild trust with their feeling body.

What is your body telling you right now about a commitment you're considering? Where do you feel expansion? Where do you feel contraction?

The Five Phases of Transformation

Based on patterns observed across hundreds of individuals and teams navigating significant transformations, I have identified five phases of transformation. This is a flexible framework that can be adapted to various contexts and challenges.

Phase 1: Recognition. This phase involves acknowledging that you stand at a threshold. The recognition might come through external circumstances, like a job loss or opportunity, or through internal knowing that something must change. The key practice in this phase is honest assessment without immediately rushing toward action. What is actually calling for transformation? What is ready to be released? What is ready to be born?

Phase 2: Preparation. Once the threshold is recognized, preparation begins. This means preparing yourself physically, emotionally, and spiritually for the journey ahead. This might involve strengthening your practice foundation, addressing unfinished business that could derail your transformation, or gathering support resources.

Phase 3: Commitment. This is the moment of stepping through the threshold. It requires a clear, embodied yes that engages your whole being. The commitment should be specific enough to guide action yet flexible enough to allow for learning and adjustment. It should be communicated to others who will be affected or who can provide support.

Phase 4: Integration. After the initial commitment, there is always a period of integration where the new way of being needs to be stabilized.

Old patterns will resurface. Unexpected challenges will emerge. This phase requires patience, self-compassion, and steady practice. The focus is on gradually establishing new neural pathways through behavioral patterns.

Phase 5: Evolution. Once the new way of being has stabilized, evolution becomes possible. From this new ground, previously invisible possibilities become apparent. The transformation that once seemed daunting becomes the foundation for the next level of growth. The cycle begins again from a higher vantage point.

Consider where you are right now. Which phase are you in with a transformation that matters to you? Are you still in recognition, sensing that something needs to change but not yet clear on what? Are you in preparation, gathering resources, and resolving old business? Have you already committed and now find yourself in the messy middle of integration? Knowing your phase helps you know what the moment actually asks of you.

Practice: Crossing the Threshold

Applied Insights

The capacity to transform commitment from an intellectual decision into an embodied action. This practice trains you to evaluate what size commitment your entire system is ready to sustain for the transformation that it initiates. Over time, you develop the ability to recognize thresholds, work skillfully with resistance, and take the first step that makes all other steps possible.

When to Use

- When you face a decision, you've been postponing
- When continued analysis is no longer serving you

- When you know what you need to do but haven't done it
- When a transformation is calling but fear keeps you at the edge
- At any significant transition point in life, work, or relationships

The Practice

Find 30-45 minutes of quiet space with a journal. This practice works best when you have a specific threshold in mind, something significant enough that crossing it will change something fundamental about your life or identity.

You'll name the threshold, work through layers of resistance, distinguish between fear of failure and fear of success, and identify the first step that transforms intention into action.

Phase One: Naming the Threshold

Write a specific statement about what commitment would mean when applied to your question. Not vague intentions but concrete reality.

What exactly would you be stepping into? What would you be leaving behind? Every threshold requires releasing something, whether it's security, familiarity, or an outdated version of yourself. It's important to stay in achievable goals, especially at the beginning. At this stage, base hits are much more valuable than attempting a home run.

What would you be stepping toward? Beyond the obvious goals, what new version of yourself would emerge? What capabilities would you need to develop? What possibilities would open that are currently closed?

Name the threshold clearly. Vague thresholds produce vague commitments.

Phase Two: Mapping Your Resistance

Using the three channels, explore what stands between you and commitment.

Body: Close your eyes and imagine having fully crossed this threshold. Where does tension emerge? What is your body trying to protect you from? What earlier experience taught your nervous system this particular fear?

Mind and Emotion: What stories arise about why now isn't the right time? Write them down. Then look beneath each story. What emotion hides behind the objection? Name it.

Intuition: Beneath the fear and the stories, what does your deeper knowing say? Is the resistance protecting you from genuine danger, or from the discomfort of growth? There's a difference between intuition saying, "not this" and fear saying, "not yet."

Now connect to your shadow work. Ask: Is any of this resistance connected to shadow material I've been avoiding? Sometimes we resist thresholds because crossing them would require integrating parts of ourselves we've disowned.

Phase Three: Upper Limit Check

This phase distinguishes between two very different types of resistance. Ask yourself: Am I afraid of failing, or am I afraid of succeeding?

Fear of failure is familiar. We resist because we might not achieve our goals, might look foolish, might lose what we have.

Fear of success is sneakier. We resist because achieving our goals would require us to become someone new, to release an identity we've outgrown, to handle more visibility or responsibility or joy than we believe we deserve.

Which fear is operating in your resistance? Be honest. Many thresholds remain uncrossed not because we doubt our ability to reach them, but because we doubt our worthiness to stand on the other side.

If you discover an upper limit operating, name specifically what you're afraid success would require of you (think of the orientation problem when we expand into larger spaces).

Phase Four: Clarifying Intent

From the work you've done, clarify what you actually want.

Write your intent in specific, concrete terms. "I want to be happier" is too vague. "I will have a conversation with my partner about what's not working in our relationship" is concrete.

Test your intent against your precepts. Does this commitment align with your true north? If there's misalignment, either revise the intent or examine whether your resistance is actually wisdom.

Ask: If I got truly clear about what I wanted, what might become visible that I haven't been able to see?

The power of clear intent is not magical. It's practical. When you know what you want, you notice opportunities that were always there but invisible to your scattered attention.

Phase Five: The First Step

Commitment becomes real through action. Identify the first step that would solidify this threshold crossing.

The step should be small enough to complete within 24 hours but significant enough to represent real change. It should be visible in some way, creating a point of no return even if that point is small.

Examples: Sending the email you've been hesitating on. Writing the first page of a project you've been waiting to start. Speaking a heartfelt truth to someone whose response you're unsure of.

Identify someone you trust to share your commitment with. Not for their approval, but for the support and accountability that comes from being witnessed. A commitment held in secret is easier to abandon.

Name your first step. Name who you'll tell. Commit to both.

Adaptations

Quick version: When facing a smaller threshold, ask only: "What am I afraid of, failure or success?" and "What's the first step I could take today?" Take that step.

Deep version: Expand Phase Two into extended journaling. Map your resistance in detail. Explore its history. Write a dialogue with the part of you that's afraid. Understand fully before you act.

Daily recommitment version: After crossing a major threshold, use a brief morning practice. Ask: "What micro-threshold do I face today that honors my larger commitment?" Identify it. Cross it.

Accountability version: Do the full practice with a trusted partner or coach who can reflect back what they hear in your resistance, help you distinguish fear from wisdom, and hold you accountable to your first step.

What to Expect

First few times: You may discover that your resistance is stronger than you realized, or that you've been confusing fear of success with fear of failure. The practice may reveal that you're not ready to cross this particular threshold, and that's useful information. Naming a threshold doesn't obligate you to cross it immediately but will help you name the steps along the way.

After a few times of doing the practice: You'll develop a clearer relationship with your own resistance patterns. You'll recognize upper limit moments more quickly. The gap between deciding and acting will shorten. You'll understand that commitment is not a single moment but a daily practice of recommitment.

Common Obstacles

"I do the practice but still don't take the first step." Look again at Phase Three. Upper limit resistance is sneaky. You may be unconsciously protecting yourself from success. Or the step you identified may be too large. Make it smaller. Make it so small that not doing it would be ridiculous.

"I'm not sure if my resistance is wisdom or fear." Fear usually has urgency, and contraction. Wisdom usually has spaciousness and clarity. Fear says "never" or "not me." Wisdom might say "not yet" or "not this way." If you're genuinely uncertain, wait. But set a date to revisit. Indefinite postponement is usually fear pretending to be wisdom.

Field Note

Nathan had been talking about leaving his corporate law career for three years. He had the financial runway. He had the idea for what he wanted to build. He had told friends and family he was "working toward" the transition. But every quarter, a new reason appeared for why this wasn't quite the right time.

When he mapped his resistance, the body scan revealed something he hadn't expected. The tension wasn't in his chest or gut where fear usually lived. It was in his hands. Tight, gripping, as if holding onto something he couldn't name.

The stories his mind offered were familiar: the market isn't right; I need one more year of savings, I should wait until after the next bonus cycle. But when he looked beneath those stories, what he found wasn't a fear of failure. He had failed before and recovered. What he found was fear of what success would require him to become.

His father had been a corporate lawyer. His grandfather, too. Three generations of men who had provided for their families by staying in structures they didn't love. To leave would mean becoming someone his family had never been. It would mean admitting that security wasn't his highest value, even though he'd been raised to believe it should be.

The upper limit wasn't about capability. It was about permission. He didn't believe he was allowed to want something different than what his lineage had chosen.

His first step was small but precise. He scheduled a conversation with his father. Not to ask permission, but to tell him the truth about what he wanted and why. He expected resistance. What he got instead was his father's quiet admission: "I always wondered what I would have built if I'd had your courage to try."

Nathan gave notice six weeks later. The threshold he'd circled for three years took less than two months to cross once he named what was actually in the way.

Remember This

The threshold is a doorway between who you have been and who you are becoming. Crossing it requires more than understanding. It requires embodied commitment that engages your whole being.

Resistance operates on three levels. Physical resistance lives in your body's protective patterns. Mental and emotional resistance hides behind rational-sounding objections. Relational resistance comes from systems that have organized themselves around who you've been. Each layer contains information about where you're attached, where your perception might be distorted, and where the real work lies.

The Upper Limit Problem explains why expansion often triggers contraction. We each carry an internal thermostat for how much success and fulfillment we allow ourselves. Crossing a threshold means building the capacity to stay in a larger space rather than unconsciously sabotaging your way back to the familiar.

Clarity precedes opportunity. Your intent directs your attention, which determines what you can see. When you get truly clear about what you want, possibilities that were always there become visible. Commitment is not a single decision, but a daily practice built through micro-commitments that train your nervous system to trust your own word.

14

WALKING YOUR PATH

"It doesn't interest me what you do for a living.
I want to know what you ache for and if you dare
to dream of meeting your heart's longing."
— Oriah Mountain Dreamer

After crossing the threshold of commitment, a new challenge emerges: How do we navigate the unfamiliar territory we have entered? The transformation we have committed to does not come with a predetermined route. There is no GPS for personal growth, no universal directions for leadership evolution. Yet we are not without guidance. Throughout human history, we have created maps to help us navigate both outer landscapes and inner transformations. These maps, when understood as living documents that evolve with our experience, become essential tools for sustaining and deepening the changes we have initiated.

The practices you have gathered throughout this book serve as reference points on your personal map. The Three-Channel Listening provides coordinates for understanding your moment-to-moment experience. The boundaries you have learned to create function like contour lines showing the shape of your terrain. The shadow work illuminates previously hidden territories. The rhythm awareness reveals the cyclical patterns of your journey. Yet these individual practices only become truly powerful when integrated into a comprehensive navigation system that you continuously update based on lived experience.

A map tells the story of how we move from one state to another. It identifies landmarks, goals, and pathways. It helps us recognize where we are, remember where we have been, and chart where we might go. But unlike the static maps we might use for geographic navigation, the maps we need for transformation must be alive, capable of evolving as we discover new territories within ourselves and our world.

Maps as Mirrors

Sometimes the most powerful maps are those created by others that serve as mirrors for our own journey. Poetry, music, stories, and art can all function as maps, encoding knowledge in forms that speak to us beyond rational understanding. These maps work not by telling us exactly where to go but by illuminating aspects of our own experience we might not otherwise recognize.

When I came across Oriah Mountain Dreamer's poem *The Invitation*, the opening lines hit me with unexpected force: "It doesn't interest me what you do for a living. I want to know what you ache for and if you dare to dream of meeting your heart's longing." My immediate reaction was defensive. I found myself cataloging all the "responsible" choices I had made, all the practical reasons for my current path. The poem had revealed, through my resistance to it, where I had compromised my deeper calling for the sake of security.

This is the gift of encountering powerful maps created by others. They reveal our current location by showing us what we resist, what we long for, and what we have forgotten. A song that moves us to tears is mapping emotional territory we may have avoided. A story that captivates us is showing us narrative patterns that resonate with our own unfolding journey. Anything can serve as a map, like the way a photograph captures a moment that reminds us of a time in our lives, and the memories, emotions, and stories of that moment unfold in our mind's eye.

The key is paying attention to these maps as they appear and recognizing that they are invitations to greater self-awareness and deeper connection with the people in your life and the world you live in. When someone shares their journey through a memoir, a teaching, or even a casual conversation, they are sharing one of their maps with us. We experience connection when we share our maps, and we increase the depth of our own understanding and our community's.

What map has recently revealed something to you? A book, a conversation, a piece of music? What did your reaction to it show you about where you are?

How Maps Reshape Us

Your mental maps are not fixed structures. They are dynamic neural networks that reshape themselves based on experience and perception. This is neuroplasticity in action. Every time you reinforce a thought pattern or behavior, you strengthen specific neural pathways. Your repeated thoughts and actions literally reshape your brain's architecture.

This contains both challenge and opportunity. The challenge is that deeply ingrained patterns, even those that no longer serve you, have carved strong pathways that your brain defaults to automatically. The opportunity is that through conscious practice, you can create new pathways that eventually become just as automatic as the old ones.

This shifts how we approach map creation. The maps you consciously create and regularly review are not just external tools. They are reshaping your neural architecture. Each time you reference your *values map* when making a decision, you strengthen pathways associated with principled action. Each time you consult your rhythm map to honor natural cycles, you reinforce patterns that support a balanced, sustainable life.

Inherited Maps

The process of creating effective personal maps begins with an honest assessment of your current navigation system. What maps are you already using, consciously or unconsciously? Most of us operate with multiple implicit maps that we have never examined directly. We carry family maps about what constitutes success or failure. We navigate with cultural maps about appropriate behavior and achievement. We reference professional maps about career progression and leadership.

These inherited and absorbed maps are not necessarily wrong, but they may not be aligned with your evolving path. The executive who unconsciously follows their father's map of what leadership looks like might find themselves forcing a style that does not match their natural strengths. The leader who has internalized cultural maps about constant growth might miss opportunities for sustainability. The first step in creating your own navigational framework is becoming conscious of the maps you are already using.

Lisa, a founder I worked with, discovered through this mapping process that she had been navigating her career using a map inherited from her immigrant parents. Their map, forged through experiences of scarcity and displacement, prioritized security above all else. Every decision she made was unconsciously filtered through the question: "Does this make me more secure?" This map had served her well in building a stable career, but it started to inhibit her from taking the strategic risks necessary for senior leadership.

Through our work together, Lisa did not discard her parents' map entirely. Security remained important to her. Instead, she created an expanded map that included security as one coordinate among several. She added coordinates for growth, contribution, and creative expression. This new, multidimensional map allowed her to make decisions that honored her need for security while also pursuing opportunities that aligned with her broader purpose.

What maps did you inherit? From your family, your culture, your mentors? Which ones still serve you, and which ones might be limiting what you can see?

Five Maps for Navigation

Creating a comprehensive navigational system requires multiple types of maps working in concert. Your values map is the lived expression of your precepts, the stars you use to orient yourself when facing hard choices. Think of it as building a navigation dashboard that provides different kinds of information for different purposes. No single map can capture the full complexity of your transformational journey, but together, multiple maps can provide the orientation you need.

Your values map serves as your moral compass, helping you maintain direction even when the path becomes unclear. This map identifies the non-negotiable principles that guide your decisions. Unlike goals, which are destinations, values are navigational stars that remain constant regardless of your specific location or circumstances.

Your capacity map tracks your resources and capabilities across different dimensions. Physical vitality, emotional resilience, mental clarity, relational support, and spiritual connection all affect your ability to navigate challenges. This map helps you recognize when you need to invest in building capacity and when you have reserves available for bold action.

Your pattern map documents recurring themes in your experience. What situations consistently trigger strong reactions? What types of challenges do you navigate successfully? Where do you repeatedly encounter similar obstacles? This map helps you recognize patterns before you are fully caught in them, allowing for earlier and more skillful intervention.

Your growth map charts the territories you are actively exploring or preparing to explore. These are the edges of your current experience, the places where you are expanding beyond familiar boundaries. This map helps you maintain intentionality about your development rather than simply responding to whatever circumstances present.

Your relationship map tracks the complex web of connections that support and challenge your growth. Who provides what kinds of support? Which relationships drain energy and which restore it? How do different people in your life relate to different aspects of your transformation? This map helps you navigate the social dimensions of change with greater skill.

Which of these five maps do you most need to create or update right now? Where is your navigation most uncertain?

Map Maintenance

Creating maps is only the beginning. For them to remain useful navigation tools, they must be regularly updated based on new experience and insights. This maintenance is an essential practice that keeps your navigation system aligned with your evolving reality.

The frequency of map maintenance depends on the type of map and your current rate of change. Your values map, once locked in, might only need review annually or during major life transitions. Your *capacity map* might benefit from monthly assessment. Your *pattern map* should be updated whenever you notice new themes or challenges. The key is establishing regular rhythms of review rather than waiting for crisis moments to reassess your navigation.

A simple approach is to create a monthly map check-in practice. At the end of every month, spend a little time reviewing and updating various maps that you're using regularly. Note what worked well, what challenges emerged, and what patterns you are noticing. This regular practice helps you catch navigational drift early, before small misalignments become major course deviations.

The practice of map maintenance also involves retiring outdated maps. The *growth map* that guided you through early career development may no longer serve you in senior leadership. The *relationship map* from before a major life transition might need complete redrawing.

Holding onto outdated maps is like trying to connect with your teenager using the same approach that worked when they were seven. The fundamental relationship is still there, but the routes to reach them have completely changed.

Maps In Relationship

While personal maps guide individual transformation, we also participate in collective maps that guide our families, communities, and the organizations we belong to. These shared frameworks emerge through the integration of multiple perspectives.

This is where the perception work from earlier in this book becomes essential. We each navigate with different maps. Your map is shaped by your experiences, your wounds, your values, your training. Someone else's map is shaped by theirs. Neither map is the territory itself. Both are interpretations.

What seems like conflict often reveals itself as different aspects of the same territory viewed from different angles. Understanding this transforms how we navigate disagreement. Rather than assuming you know what someone else sees, ask the question: What map are they using? What does their vantage point reveal that mine cannot? This simple shift moves you from defending your map, to creating a deeper connection and more complete picture of the territory you share.

Practice: The Compass

Applied Insights

The capacity to integrate what resonated with you in this book into a sustainable navigation system. This practice helps you to orient to your precepts, read your five maps, maintain daily and monthly rhythms of growth, and continuously recalibrate as you change. Over time, the compass becomes internalized, guiding your decisions and actions without requiring conscious effort.

When to Use

- As your primary ongoing practice after completing this book
- When you feel lost or disconnected from your direction
- When circumstances have shifted and you need to reorient
- At the beginning or ending of any new chapter of life, work, or relationship
- Monthly: reflection and recalibration
- Daily: brief orientation

The Practice

Take as long as you need for the initial setup of your compass practice, then check in monthly with the compass to make sure you're on the path. Reflect daily to check in with the local steps on your path. This keeps the whole and its parts present enough that you'll stay on track. This practice assumes you have already identified your five precepts. If you haven't, return to that practice before proceeding.

Phase One: Orientation

Begin by reconnecting with your precepts. Read them aloud or write them out. These are your fixed stars, the principles that remain constant regardless of circumstances.

Then assess your current position using the five maps:

Values Map: How aligned are your current actions with your precepts? Where are you living your values? Where have you drifted? What change will help create more balance?

Capacity Map: What are your current resources? Physical energy, emotional resilience, mental clarity, time, and support. Where are you resourced? Where are you depleted? Rate your overall capacity from one to ten.

Pattern Map: What recurring themes are showing up in your life right now? What patterns from earlier chapters are you working with? What shadows are active? What perceptual habits are influencing how you see?

Growth Map: What territory are you currently exploring? What edge are you at? What are you learning? What skills or capacities are you developing? Which is most important at present?

Relationship Map: How are your key relationships right now? Where is there a connection and support? Where is there friction or distance? How are you showing up for others?

Write brief notes on each map. This gives you your current coordinates.

Phase Two: Direction

From your orientation, identify your primary focus for this period. You can't work on everything at once. Choose one area that most needs your attention.

Ask: Given where I am and what my precepts say matters, what is the most important focus for the next week and the next three months?

This might be a specific threshold you're crossing, a pattern you're working with, a relationship that needs attention, or a capacity you're building.

Name your primary direction clearly. Write it as a specific intention.

Then ask: Which practice most supports this direction? You might need to return to shadow work, or boundary mapping, or the stillness cascade, or the adaptive response. Let your direction guide which tools you use.

Phase Three: Daily Practice

Design a daily structure that supports your current direction. This doesn't need to be elaborate. Consistency matters more than duration.

Morning orientation (2-5 minutes): Reconnect with your precepts and your current direction. Ask: How will I honor these today? What one thing would make this day aligned?

Engaged action: Dedicated time for whatever practice supports your current direction. If you're working on shadow material, this might be journaling. If you're building stillness, this might be the cascade practice. If you're crossing a threshold, this might be taking concrete steps. Match the practice to your direction.

Evening reflection: Notice what happened. Where did you stay aligned? Where did you drift? What did you learn? This isn't self-judgment. It's data collection, a clear mirror for navigation.

Write down what your daily structure will be. Keep it simple enough that you'll actually do it.

Phase Four: Monthly Reflection

Set aside time each month for deeper reflection and recalibration. This is your map maintenance session.

Review the month through your five maps:

What worked well? What practices supported your alignment?

What challenged you? What activated your resistance or shadows?

What patterns emerged? What are you noticing about yourself?

What needs to change? Does your direction need adjustment? Does your daily practice need modification?

Write your insights. Over time, these monthly reflections become a new map of your growth, showing you how far you've traveled and revealing patterns that aren't visible day to day.

Phase Five: Accountability

Growth accelerates when witnessed. Identify at least one person with whom you'll share your compass work.

Share your precepts and your current direction. Ask them to check in with you periodically. Give them permission to ask hard questions. The right witness will support your growth without letting you off the hook.

This isn't about seeking approval or reporting to an authority. It's about the power of being seen in your commitment.

If you don't have someone who can serve this role, consider finding a coach, joining a growth-oriented community, or creating a reciprocal accountability partnership with someone else doing similar work.

Adaptations

Quick daily version (5 minutes): Read your precepts. Ask: "What's my one priority today that honors my direction?" Check in briefly at day's end.

Deep quarterly version (2-3 hours): Full reassessment of all five maps. Review your monthly reflections for patterns. Adjust your direction for the coming quarter. Update your precepts if your understanding has deepened.

Crisis version: When you feel completely lost, return to Phase One only. Reconnect with your precepts. Assess your five maps honestly. Often, orientation alone reveals the next step.

Partner version: Do the full practice with your accountability partner. Share your maps. Reflect together. Mutual witnessing deepens the work for both.

What to Expect

First few times: The practice may feel elaborate or time-consuming. You may struggle to assess some maps honestly. The daily structure may feel forced. This is normal. You're building a new habit of intentional navigation. Start with the minimum and build from there.

After a few times of doing the practice: The orientation becomes faster. You'll know your maps well enough to assess them quickly. The daily rhythm becomes natural. You'll notice when you've drifted before the drift becomes serious. The compass starts working in the background, informing decisions without requiring formal practice.

Common Obstacles

"I don't have time for all this." Start with the daily orientation only. Five minutes in the morning, two minutes at night. Add monthly reflection when that's stable. The full practice is the destination, not

the starting point. Something small and consistent beats something elaborate and abandoned.

"I keep forgetting to do it." Anchor the practice to something you already do. Morning orientation with your coffee. Evening reflection before bed. Monthly review on the last Sunday of the month. Use your environment to remind you. Put your precepts where you'll see them.

Field Note

Oren was a filmmaker whose work focused on creating deeper connections between people. He had developed a unique way of filming two people in conversations that helped them enter into uncharted intimacy using only five questions. The results were remarkable.

When he came to see me, his company was on the brink of implosion. His passion for the work was complete, and the work itself was valuable, but he couldn't see what was in the way.

We began setting up his compass by going through the precepts and the five maps. As we worked through his precepts, it became clear that caring for others was central to how he led. But in Oren's case, he carried a shadow with this value that was distorting it. His sense of responsibility for others was fueled by guilt about his own fortune and capacity.

When we matched the shadow to the value, we discovered he had been overcompensating. He was keeping people in his company and maintaining its size when it needed to be streamlined to survive. He felt responsible for the lives of everyone who worked with him. That sense of responsibility was also holding his team in a pattern of feeling like they weren't able to succeed as well.

It's often the case when our shadows rule our values that we find ourselves unknowingly ensnaring others in our shadow's trap. Oren had forgotten to apply his value of caring for others to himself.

We were having dinner at an Indian restaurant during our last session together. As he talked through what he was seeing, the emotion caught up with him. He had been holding on to caring for all of these people, and because of that, he was actually diminishing their potential. Everyone was going down together on a sinking ship.

Then something shifted. A lightness came over his face. He realized he didn't have to carry that burden any longer.

Once he let go, he moved quickly. He shrunk the company to 25% of what it had been, supporting everyone through the transition. The company began to accelerate and grow. Within two years, he had hired back most of the people he had let go, creating a future that was sustainable for them and for the business.

To this day, he maintains his compass through brief practices in the morning. When there's a life change, we do a deeper dive together. The maintenance has kept him on track.

Remember This

Maps for transformation are living documents that must evolve as you discover new territories within yourself and your world. Unlike static guides that become obsolete, living maps grow richer and more accurate through continuous revision based on actual experience. Your mental maps are dynamic neural networks that reshape themselves through neuroplasticity. Every time you reference your values when making decisions or honoring your natural rhythms, you strengthen neural pathways that make these navigational patterns increasingly automatic.

Multiple types of maps must work in concert. Your *values map* provides moral direction. Your *capacity map* tracks resources. Your *pattern map* reveals recurring themes. Your *growth map* charts territories you are exploring. Your *relationship map* illuminates the social dimensions of change. No single map captures the full complexity of transformation, but together they provide the orientation needed for skillful navigation.

We each navigate with different maps shaped by different experiences. What seems like conflict often reveals itself as different aspects of the same territory viewed from different angles. Rather than defending your map, ask: What map are they using? What does their vantage point reveal that mine cannot? The maps created by others, through poetry, music, art, story, or action, serve as mirrors that reveal aspects of our own journey we might not otherwise recognize.

Your precepts serve as your true north, the fixed coordinates that keep you oriented regardless of shifting landscapes. The Compass integrates everything in this book into a sustainable system: daily orientation, engaged action, monthly reflection, and ongoing accountability. This is not a path you complete but a cycle you continue for the rest of your life. The practices in this book have given you tools. The Compass you create from here forward is yours alone. It will guide you through territories no one else can chart, toward a life that only you can live.

ABOUT THE AUTHOR

Thomas Droge has spent three decades where few people have stood: inside both the meditation hall and the boardroom. A physician of classical Chinese medicine, Qigong master, Daoist, and leadership coach, He has worked with Fortune 500 leaders, professional athletes, artists, and high-growth tech founders — and spent the past four years as Chief Mindfulness Officer at TIFIN, a billion-dollar AI and fintech incubator, where he worked alongside founders and leaders building organizations from the inside out.

Trained at Pacific College of Oriental Medicine, Jiangxi College in China, and Harvard's Benson-Henry Institute for Mind Body Medicine, Droge has taught and treated thousands — from patients navigating late-stage illness to leaders navigating high-stakes decisions.

The Leader Within is the distillation of everything he has learned about what actually transforms people: not better thinking, but deeper knowing.

www.ingramcontent.com/pod-product-compliance
Lightning Source LLC
LaVergne TN
LVHW010647110826
845149LV00014B/2986

* 9 7 9 8 9 9 5 0 4 0 9 1 0 *